CHRIST'S APOSTLE

Representing Jesus

ROBERT MAASBACH

Grosvenor House
Publishing Limited

This book is published by
Grosvenor House Publishing Ltd
Link House
140 The Broadway, Tolworth, Surrey, KT6 7HT.
www.grosvenorhousepublishing.co.uk

A CIP record for this book
is available from the British Library

ISBN 978-1-78623-587-9

Bible Quotations

On many occasions Bible verses and phrases have been paraphrased by the author, and are not intended as an exact rendering of recognised translations. Scripture references are given for further study.

The following versions of the Bible have been used in this book:

AMP stands for the *Amplified Bible*
AMPC stands for the *Amplified Classic Bible*
NCV stands for *New Century Version*
NET stands for *New English Translation*
NKJV stands for *New King James Version*
NLT stands for the *New Living Translation*
TEV stands for *Today's English Version / Good News Bible*
TLB stands for *The Living Bible*

CONTENTS

PROLOGUE   vii

PART 1   **CHRIST'S APOSTLE**   1

Chapter 1   A Body You have Prepared for Me   3

Chapter 2   The Seed of the Woman   11

Chapter 3   The Seed of Abraham   16

Chapter 4   The Seed of David   20

Chapter 5   What is an Apostle?   26

PART 2   **PETER, CHRIST'S APOSTLE**   29

Chapter 6   Christ Appointed, not Self-Appointed   31

Chapter 7   The Word and The Spirit   39

Chapter 8   Preaching and Protecting the Gospel   50

Chapter 9   Christ's Love in Marriage   59

Chapter 10   The Father's Provision   65

PART 3   **JOHN, CHRIST'S APOSTLE**   71

Chapter 11   The Father's Love   73

Chapter 12   A Tender Heart   86

Chapter 13   Opening Blind Eyes   97

Chapter 14   Growing in Grace   112

Chapter 15   Seeing Christ Glorified   119

PART 4   PAUL, CHRIST'S APOSTLE   123

Chapter 16   Proclaiming the Life-giving Gospel   125

Chapter 17   The Joy of the Lord   139

Chapter 18   Building on the Right Foundation   150

Chapter 19   We do not get Discouraged   163

Chapter 20   Radiant with the Light of His Life   175

PROLOGUE

The Life I now live is not my own, it is a gift of God, given through Jesus Christ - Who is my Life! Because of this, life on earth would seem meaningless unless I spent it in the joy of serving Him who loves me and gives me His Life. Saying this, I believe that in writing this book I have served the Lord Jesus and I am deeply grateful for the privilege to share this with you.

My prayer for you is that as you read, the Holy Spirit will help you to see the Father in His Son Jesus, and that you would see who He has made you in Him, and all that He gives you through Him. I also pray that you are continually filled with the richest measure of His Divine presence, so that your whole spirit, soul and body are filled and flooded with God Himself.

When I use the term "Christ's Apostle", I am simply referring to a representative of Jesus. Of course, all God's children are His representatives and will therefore be enriched by reading this book, because they will see what they are freely given in Jesus. However, I am also writing this for those whom God has specifically called, chosen and sent to represent His Son Jesus in the work of ministering as His Apostles.

To understand what an Apostle is, you need to know who Jesus is, for He is the perfect Apostle of God. The wonder of His Apostleship has such a glorious foundation in God that you cannot but be in awe when you look at Jesus. He who came forth from the bosom of the intimate presence of the Father, He has revealed Him in the body prepared for Him, so that we might find, know and see the only true Living God in Him. Jesus, the Son of God, is the Son of Man, and not just any man - He is the promised Seed of the woman, the Promised Seed of Abraham and the promised

Seed of David. He came in fulfilment to God's Word, the inspired scriptures, and in Him we can see the fullness of God bodily. And not only that, but in Jesus you can also see whom God has predestined you to be - for you are "in Him, made full and having come to fullness of Life [in Christ you too are filled with the Godhead - Father, Son and Holy Spirit - and reach full spiritual stature]" (Colossians 2:10 AMPC).

After laying the foundation of who Jesus is, you will read about Peter, John and Paul's Apostleship. Firstly, how God made Peter Christ's Apostle. How satan opposed God's will concerning Peter, but how through his union with Jesus, God's Word prevailed in him. How as Christ's Apostle, filled with the Holy Spirit and power, Peter trampled the forces of darkness under his feet, in a highly political and religious environment, as he masterfully opened the scriptures to show that Jesus is the Christ, the Son of the Living God. Jesus enabled Peter to give His saving grace to multitudes of precious souls by giving them His Life. There are many things by which you can see Peter is Christ's Apostle, but fundamentally he is an Apostle because the Father revealed in him that Jesus is the Christ, the Son of the Living God.

Next you will see how John became Christ's Apostle, and how in the time of his preparation, the Father was able to form the tender heart of Jesus in him, whereby he was able to see what the Father desires to show you and me. John's Apostleship stands out with such glorious Light of Life that you can clearly see the Father in the Son. And Christ's Apostle John was also given the immeasurable privilege to show us not only Jesus in His resurrected body, but also in His glorified body in heaven.

Finally, you will see how God made Paul Christ's Apostle. To Paul - who felt he was born almost too late for this and unworthy to be called an Apostle - the love and kindness of God was revealed when he met Jesus. Paul says,

"But by the grace of God I am what I am, and His grace toward me was not in vain; but I laboured more abundantly than they all, yet not I, but the grace of God which was with me" (1 Corinthians 15:10). Paul did not walk with Jesus like Peter and John did, but what is so encouraging, is that he did not know Jesus any less intimately. I say this so that you may know that because you love Jesus, He will reveal Himself in you, so that you too may make Him known in all you are, say and do by the power of the Holy Spirit.

I pray that "the God of peace [Who is the Author and the Giver of peace], Who brought again from among the dead our Lord Jesus, that great Shepherd of the sheep, by the blood [that sealed, ratified] the everlasting agreement [covenant, testament], strengthen, (complete, perfect) and make you what you ought to be and equip you with everything good that you may carry out His will; [while He Himself] works in you and accomplishes that which is pleasing in His sight, through Jesus Christ (the Messiah); to Whom be the glory forever and ever (to the ages of the ages). Amen (so be it)" (Hebrews 13:20-21 AMPC).

Part 1
CHRIST'S APOSTLE

Chapter 1

A BODY YOU HAVE PREPARED FOR ME

"Therefore, when He came into the world, He said, 'Sacrifice and offering You did not desire, but a body You have prepared for Me.' Then I said, 'Behold, I have come - In the volume of the book it is written of Me. To do Your will, O God.' By that will we have been sanctified through the offering of the body of Jesus Christ once for all" (Hebrews 10:5,7,10).

To understand what an Apostle is, you need to know who Jesus is, for He is the perfect Apostle of God.

The Perfect Apostle

The wonder of Apostleship has such a glorious foundation in God that you cannot but be in awe when you look at Jesus Christ, for He is the perfect Apostle of God. He is the visible image of the invisible God. He came forth from the Father - was sent by Him to reveal Him - so we can see God in all Jesus is, says and does. Jesus Christ alone is the foundation of true Apostleship in creation, for He is the sole expression of the glory of God - the Light-being, the out-raying, the radiance of the divine - He is the perfect imprint and very image of God's nature. In Jesus we see the fullness of God the Father, the Son and Holy Spirit perfectly One in the body prepared for Him.

The Fall of Men

Now consider this, that in the beginning God said, "Let Us make man in Our image, according to Our likeness; Let them

3

have dominion." So, God created man in His own image; in the image of God He created him; male and female He created them. And God blessed them (Genesis 1:26-28).

The first man, Adam, was given a body which God formed from the dust of the ground. God then breathed into his nostrils the breath of Life, and man became a living being - "a living soul." Sometime later, God caused a deep sleep to fall on Adam, and while he slept, He took one of his ribs and closed up the flesh in its place. Then the rib which the Lord God had taken from the man He made into a woman, and He brought her to the man. Adam then said, "This is now bone of my bones and flesh of my flesh; she shall be called woman, because she was taken out of man." Therefore, a man shall leave his father and mother and be joined to his wife, and they shall become one flesh (Genesis 2:7, 21-24).

The woman, having been deceived by the devil, was given a promise of redemption when God said to the devil that her Seed (Jesus), "shall bruise your head, and you shall bruise His heel." This bruising of the heel refers to the suffering of Jesus on the Cross, for "He was bruised for our iniquities" (Genesis 3:15; Isaiah 53:5).

What is very important to see is that before the woman was formed, God said to Adam, "Of the tree of the knowledge of good and evil you shall not eat, for in the day that you eat of it you shall surely die" (Genesis 2:17). It was because Adam disobeyed God that the glory of His Life faded in him as the law of sin and death entered him. Therefore, Adam became self-conscious instead of being God-conscious.

Consider the power of the law of sin and death in men, how it separates us from God so that His glorious image is not visible, and we no longer represent and emanate the Light of the Life of Him who made us. You can see that because this one man Adam sinned, the sin nature was passed on to every human being, for it is written, "All have sinned and fall short of the glory of God" (Romans 3:23). This is a great mystery that affects us all, for we all bear the image of the first man, Adam, who is a type of Him - Jesus - who was to come. It was because Adam sinned that we all die and because of him we are by nature self-conscious, or I should say, sin-conscious rather than God-conscious. You see, sin is what separates us from God.

The Good News

But God who is rich in mercy, because of the great love with which He loves us, sent His Son Jesus Christ from heaven to become the Son of Man. He, being the form of God, became Man by taking on the body God prepared for Him, so that all could see the glory of His Life with the Father as His only begotten Son; a Life full of the Father's loving grace and truth. The good news is that all who receive Jesus are given His Life-giving power to become sons and daughters of God and have a new birth through His Life in them; so that just as we have borne the image of the natural man, Adam, so now we are given to bear the image of the heavenly Man, Jesus, and are given Eternal Life in Him.

I pray as you read this book that you may really come to know practically, through experience for yourself, the love of Jesus Christ as all God's children should - how long, how wide, how deep, and how high His love really is - and live in His love, so that you are filled through all your being with the fullness of God and may have the richest measure of His divine Presence and become a body wholly filled and flooded with God Himself.

In Jesus you can clearly see what this looks like, to be a body wholly filled and flooded with God Himself. "For in Him dwells all the fullness of the Godhead bodily" (Colossians 2:9). Jesus came from heaven and took upon Himself the body God prepared for Him. And when He was found in appearance as a Man, He perfectly unveiled the image of God the Father. However, Jesus not only unveiled the Father, but in Himself He also reveals what you are predestined and called to be.

Beloved, think about the riches of the glory of God's grace. The Life you see in Jesus, He now gives to live in you. For this is the love of the Father for you, that Jesus bore in His body, once and for all, our sins and sicknesses on the Cross, and suffered God's wrath against sin in His death. He paid our debt in full. Jesus perfectly unveiled the Father's love for us, not only in His nature, but in the action of His obedience to fulfil all that is written.

The Psalmist refers to the Man, Christ Jesus, when he says by the inspiration of the Holy Spirit - "What is man that You are mindful of him and would visit him? And who is this Son of Man that You think so highly of Him to place all things under His feet?" (Psalm 8; Psalm 144; 1 Corinthians 15; Hebrews 2). Jesus is this Man, for He gave Himself to God to put away the power of sin once and for all by dying for you so that now He can demonstrate His power over sin and death by justifying you freely by God's grace.

And remember this: where sins have been forever forgiven and forgotten, there is nothing you need to do to get rid of them, but believe upon the Lord Jesus Christ and in repentance turn to Him by being water baptised into His death, so that you may arise to newness of Life with Him and live through His Life in you to the glory of God. Now therefore look to Jesus, the author and finisher of your faith, for in His loving-kindness He gives you a new spiritually alive heart so that you will want what God wants, and He gives you a new spiritually alive mind so you will know what He wants. Through Jesus you will know God inwardly and by the help of the Holy Spirit you will be able to draw near to Him and worship Him in truth.

With these thoughts in mind, consider the greatness of what Jesus has accomplished for you. He has opened the way for you to draw near to the Father by tearing the curtain of His human body on the Cross, through shedding His precious blood when He died, so as to forever remove the separation between you and the Father when He rose again. Jesus lives forever and is faithful to completely cleanse and perfect you, as He leads you through His Spirit into the very holy of holies, into the bosom of the intimate presence of the Father, the place from which He came forth, to which He in Himself is the Way, for there He ever lives to make intercession, to provide you a warm welcome in the presence of the Father.

I therefore pray that you may know the Holy Spirit today drawing you up to where Jesus is, making you perfectly acceptable and well-pleasing to the Father by revealing Himself in you. Now this is what is called amazing grace! How sweet the sound that saved a wretch like me, Amen!

Jesus gave Himself to God for You

In all the wonders of God's nature and glory that Jesus came to unveil in Himself, He wants you to see, how, by the virtue of His Eternal Spirit, He offered Himself without blemish to God for you. This is so that you can receive through faith the power in His precious blood to free your conscience from dead works, which is that inward Adamic sin-nature that motivates you to do those things that makes you die spiritually and separates you from God.

Beloved, these are the riches of the glory of God's grace that you receive in Jesus. So that now by the same power through which He gave His Life, He enables you to die with Him to sin; and that by the same power through which He rose again, Jesus enables you to live through Him to the glory of God (John 10:17-18).

Let me say this again so that it may deeply penetrate your heart: Jesus - by virtue of His Eternal Spirit, His own pre-existent divine personality - gave Himself to God for you. He, being the perfect Son of God, shining forth the Light of His Life, shed His precious blood to provide the purchase price by which God can redeem you. What this means is that Jesus bought your freedom from the power of sin - and He is perfectly able to liberate you from that inward motivation that leads to spiritual death and separation from the Light of His Life.

So, you can see why Christ's blood gives God the right to justify you freely by His grace and declare you "not guilty" in His sight. Yes, it is God's great pleasure to reconcile you to Himself by not imputing your sins. Why? Because Jesus bore them all.

Oh, how great is the Father's love for us in Jesus, that He now gives and maintains His Life in us so that we may belong to Him inwardly forever, knowing, perceiving and recognising within us and others the wonder of His person, shining ever more brightly with the Light of His Life until that perfect day when we see Jesus and are made perfect in His likeness.

Now all the honour belongs to God the Father of our Lord Jesus Christ for giving us the privilege to be born again and become a member of His family in heaven and those who are still on earth! And because you are now His child, you have become a partaker of His divine nature, His character, His goodness and His glory.

The Life I now Live is not my own

I pray that you are encouraged as you read about these wonderful truths, and through faith enjoy the rich experience of the Father's love for you. Never forget that His Holy

Spirit is at work in you, cleansing you with the blood of Jesus, making you well-pleasing in His sight. This is why you now desire what is good and right and shun what is evil, for you are living a new Life, a heavenly Life, a holy sinless Life. This Life is kept in heaven, pure and undefiled, beyond the reach of change and decay in the body of Jesus and is continually given to you freely by God's grace through Jesus, who is your Life.

Do you see it? The Life you now live in the body is not your own; it is a gift of God! And this Life was made manifest in all its fullness in the body of Jesus, Who showed Himself to be triumphant over sin and death. Jesus said, "I am the resurrection and the Life. I am He who lives, and was dead, and behold, I am alive forevermore. Everyone who believes in Me has Eternal Life and even though he may die yet he shall live, 'Do not fear, for I have the keys of Hades and of Death'" (John 11:25; John 3:36; Revelation 1:18).

This Jesus, who became the Son of Man, who suffered, died and rose again, is now revealed by the power of an endless Life as the Son of God at His right hand. He is the Heir of the promised blessing of the Father, having received the Holy Spirit who proceeds from the Father (Acts 2:33).

Remember, Jesus said, "If anyone thirsts, let him come to Me and drink. He who believes in Me, as the Scripture has said, out of his heart will flow rivers of living water." But this He spoke concerning the Spirit, whom those believing in Him would receive; for the Holy Spirit was not yet given, because Jesus was not yet glorified (John 7:37-39).

I pray as you read this, your heart rejoices as does mine while I am writing these glorious things. For God, who is rich in mercy, longs to be merciful to you so that He may satisfy the great love He feels for you by making you - who were spiritually dead - alive with Jesus. It is therefore the joy of the Lord Jesus to see the fruit of His travail - His suffering, by continually recreating you in the image of Himself inwardly; unceasingly giving His Eternal Life of Sonship in your spirit so that as He lives, you may live also. Jesus said, "Because I live you will live also, for as the living Father sent Me, and I live because of the Father, so he who feeds on Me will live because of Me" (John 14:19, 6:57).

Selah.

Take a moment and worshipfully meditate on this and the Holy Spirit will refresh you in your union with the Father and the Son, who is Jesus Christ our Lord.

Chapter 2

THE SEED OF THE WOMAN

I trust you are beginning to see the handiwork of God - how He prepared a body for Jesus - and why it is so important that Jesus, being perfectly God, is perfectly the Son of Man; and not just any man, but the One promised and foreshadowed in scripture. For the first man Adam was of the earth, made of the dust, through whom sin entered the world and by whom all die. But Jesus Christ is the Lord from heaven. He, being the form of God, is now perfectly revealed in the body God prepared for Him. In Him the mystery of godliness is unveiled, for in Him we see God in the body, and by Him we all receive Eternal Life.

The Son of God is the Son of Man

Now consider that in the fullness of time, the angel Gabriel visited Mary, being a virgin, who was given the immeasurable grace to bear the Seed, for she received the Word of the Lord saying, "Behold, you will conceive in your womb and bring forth a Son, and shall call His name Jesus, for He will save His people from their sins." All this was done that it might be fulfilled which was spoken by the Lord through the prophet, saying, "Behold, the virgin shall be with child, and bear a Son, and they shall call His name Immanuel, which is translated, 'God with us'. He will be great and will be called the Son of the Highest; and the Lord God will give Him the throne of His father David. And He will reign over the house of Jacob forever, and of His kingdom there will be no end." Then Mary said to the angel, "How can this be, since I do not know a man?" And the angel answered and said to her, "The Holy Spirit will come upon you, and the power of the Highest will overshadow you; therefore, also, that Holy One who is to be born will be called the Son of God. Now indeed, Elizabeth your relative has also conceived a son in her old age, and this is now the sixth month for her who was called barren. For with God nothing will be impossible." Then Mary said, "Behold the maidservant of the Lord! Let it be to me according to your word." And the angel departed from her (Matthew 1:20-23; Luke 1:31-38).

It is very important you understand why Jesus had to be born of the Seed of the woman - so that He might come according to the Seed of the ever-living Word of God which said, "Her Seed, He shall bruise your head, and you shall bruise His heel." You see, God does all things in fulfilment of His Word (Genesis 3:15).

King David, speaking prophetically about the body God prepared for Jesus, said, "You saw my bones being formed as I took shape in my mother's body. When I was put together there, you saw my body as it was formed. And in Your book they all were written, the days fashioned for me, when as yet there were none of them" (Psalm 139:15-16 NCV/NKJV). John shows the wonder of God preparing a body for Jesus when he says, "And the Word (Christ) became flesh (human, incarnate) and tabernacled (fixed His tent of flesh, lived awhile) among us; and we [actually] saw His glory (His honour, His majesty), such glory as an only begotten son receives from his father, full of grace (favour, loving-kindness) and truth" (John 1:14 AMPC).

In Jesus you see how God the Father opened His bosom, His intimate presence, out of which He brought forth His only begotten Son. Jesus is the visible image of the invisible God. He existed before all things and by Him all things were created that are in heaven and on earth, visible and invisible.

All things were created through Him and for Him. He is before all things, and in Him all things consist and are held together. He is and was and is to come, the Alpha and the Omega, the Beginning and the End, the Almighty. He is the One of whom it is written, "For unto us a Child is born, unto us a Son is given; and the government will be upon His shoulder. And His name will be called Wonderful, Counsellor, Mighty God, Everlasting Father, Prince of Peace" (Isaiah 9:6).

Jesus Christ is the faithful witness, the firstborn from the dead, and the ruler over the kings of the earth. And of the increase of His government and peace there will be no end. Upon the throne of David and over His kingdom, to order it and establish it with judgment and justice from that time forward, even forever. The zeal of the Lord of hosts will perform this.

The True Spirit of Apostleship

Jesus shines with God's glory and all that He is and does marks Him as God. It is for this reason that Jesus is the true Spirit of Apostleship, for He came forth from the Father and was sent by Him to reveal Him and to help us find and know the only true Living God in Him. Remember when He was transfigured, how His face shone like the sun and His clothes became as white as the light, and the Father's majestic voice was heard saying, "This is My Beloved Son, in whom I am well pleased. Hear Him!" (Matthew 17:1-5).

Without Jesus all we would have to see of the image of God are shadows and types. While these are precious and gave hope to those who lived under the old covenant, we, through faith in Jesus, now live in the substance of the things they hoped for and the evidence of what they could not see; for we now see God the Father in Jesus. Jesus said, "He who has seen Me has seen the Father. Blessed are your eyes for they see, and your ears for they hear; for assuredly, I say to you that many prophets and righteous men desired to see what you see, and did not see it, and to hear what you hear, and did not hear it" (John 14:9; Matthew 13:16-17). Therefore, look to Jesus, the Apostle of our faith, the giver of faith and the One who sustains our faith, for He unveiled the Father in the body prepared for Him.

This is the true Spirit of Apostleship - that the Father Himself bears witness of His Son! Jesus said, "The Father Himself who sent Me, has testified of Me and I know the witness which He witnesses of Me is true. All things have been delivered to Me by My Father, and no one knows the Son except the Father. Nor does anyone know the Father except the Son, and the one to whom the Son wills to reveal Him" (John 5:32, 36-37; Matthew 11:27).

Look to Jesus

When you consider the true Spirit of Apostleship, you need to look to Jesus, who is the Apostle and High Priest of our confession. He is the One who loved us and washed us from our sins in His own blood and has made us kings and priests to His God and Father. To Him be glory and dominion forever and ever, Amen!

God's glory and dominion is revealed in Jesus who is faithful to Him who put all things under His feet and appointed Him the universal and supreme Head of the Church (a headship exercised throughout the Church). The Church is His body, the fullness of Him Who fills all in all, for in that body lives the full measure of Him Who makes everything complete, and Who fills everything everywhere with Himself (Psalm 8:6; Ephesians 1:22-23).

Behold, Jesus is coming with clouds, and every eye will see Him, even they who pierced Him, and all the tribes of the earth will mourn because of Him. Even so, Amen! When Jesus returns, God will bring back with Him all the Christians who have died (1 Thessalonians 4:14 LB); and we who remain and have been made alive with Him will be made perfect in His likeness, when we see Him. In the twinkling of an eye we will be changed and made glorious with His glory, perfected as He is reflected in us, when He presents us to the Father holy, acceptable and well pleasing in His sight. To God be the glory in the Church by Christ Jesus to all generations, forever and ever, Amen! (Ephesians 3:21).

Selah.
Take a moment and worshipfully meditate on this and the Holy Spirit will refresh you in your union with the Father and the Son, who is Jesus Christ our Lord.

Chapter 3

THE SEED OF ABRAHAM

When God Almighty called Abraham, He gave him the promise of immense blessings and preached the Gospel to him, saying, "In you all the nations, families and kindred of the earth shall be blessed [and by you they will bless themselves]" (Genesis 12:1-3; Galatians 3:8 AMPC).

Powerful Prophetic Revelation

After being called by God, Abraham met Melchizedek. The word Melchi means, "My king" and the word Zedek means "righteousness". So the word Melchizedek means, "My king of righteousness". Now Melchizedek was the king of Salem, which later was called Jerusalem. Salem signifies "to make whole, complete, or perfect"; it denotes "peace" - making whole the breaches in the political and domestic union of kingdoms, states, families; the ending of discord, and the establishing of friendship.

There is no record of Melchizedek's father or mother, or of any of his ancestors - no record of his birth or of his death. He was made like the Son of God; remaining a priest forever. In Melchizedek God gives one of the most powerful prophetic revelations in scripture, for like Jesus, he is called a priest of God Most High and a minister of His righteousness, peace and joy in the anointing of a Life that has no beginning or end (Hebrews 7:3; Psalm 110:4).

Melchizedek brought out bread and wine and blessed Abraham who had the promise saying, "Blessed be Abram of God Most High, Possessor of heaven and earth; and blessed be God Most High, who has delivered your enemies into your hand." And Abraham gave him a tithe of all (Genesis 14:19-20). This High-priestly blessing enabled Abraham to see what God had prepared in heaven to be fulfilled on earth through his Seed. You see, God showed Abraham that through his Seed - Jesus - He would bring many sons to glory, those who would be born of the Spirit, who would no longer be strangers and foreigners to heaven, but citizens and members of the household of God - as many as the stars in the heavens, and as innumerable as the grains of sand by the sea.

It is very important you see God working when He called Abraham, who was seventy-five years old, and said to him, "I will make you". Then when Abraham was ninety-nine years old, God appeared to him again and said, "I am Almighty God (All-powerful, All-sufficient, eternally capable of being all you need), walk before Me and be blameless. No longer shall your name be called Abram (exalted father), but your name shall be Abraham (father of a multitude), for "I have made you" a father of many nations (Genesis 12:2, 17:1,5). God filled Abraham, through His all-sufficient Spirit of grace, with hope against hope, so that with joy and peace in believing he had the blessed assurance that God was fulfilling His Word. Through His Word God formed, created in Abraham's heart, His gift of faith.

Faith through His Promise and His Oath

By faith Abraham understood that the things God promised, which were naturally impossible and invisible, would become possible and visible by His Word; for he stood in the presence of God in whom he believed, so that he became the father of many nations, according to what was spoken, "So shall your descendants be."

The faith God gave Abraham through His ever-living Word never grew weak, even though his own body was as good as dead, since he was about a hundred years old and Sarah's womb had never known life. Abraham did not waver at the promise of God through unbelief, but rather was strengthened in faith, giving glory to God because he was fully convinced that what God had promised, He was also able to perform. Therefore by faith he was accounted righteous, living in right-standing with God (Romans 4:17-22). It is therefore written that from this one man, Abraham, a man as good as dead, from his Seed - Jesus - were born as many as the stars in the sky in multitude and as innumerable as the sand by the seashore (Hebrews 11:12).

I say all of this so that you may be able to see why Jesus is the true Spirit of Apostleship, for the body God prepared for Him was not fashioned by human will, desire or ability. God clearly shows through His Word and works that Jesus is foreknown and predestined to come through Abraham to bless us all with His Eternal Life of Sonship. Remember, Jesus said, "Most assuredly, I say to you, before Abraham was, I AM." And, "Abraham rejoiced to see My day (My incarnation, being revealed in the body), and he saw it and was glad" (John 8:58, 56).

The Holy Spirit is here to open your understanding to the true Spirit of Apostleship, which has its foundation in God, who speaks His Word of promise with such certainty that it leaves no question as to its fulfilment. For God desired to show Abraham - who was to inherit the promise - more convincingly and beyond all doubt the unchangeable nature of His promise. It is for this reason that God intervened and mediated His promise with an oath, saying, "By Myself I have sworn, says the Lord. Blessing I will bless you, and multiplying, I will multiply your descendants as the stars of the heaven and as the sand which is on the seashore. And your descendants shall possess the gate of their enemies. In your Seed - Jesus - all the nations of the earth shall be blessed, because you have obeyed My voice" (Genesis 22:16-19).

Can you see the blessed assurance God gives by His promise and His oath?! You see by these two unchangeable things - in which it is impossible for God ever to prove false or deceive us - we, who have fled to Him for refuge, have a mighty indwelling strength and strong encouragement to grasp and hold fast the ever-living hope for an Eternal Life of sonship appointed for us and set before us in Jesus (Hebrews 6:17-18).

No Apostleship outside of Jesus

So you see, Jesus is not only the Seed of the woman, but He is also the Seed of Abraham. His coming in the body is the promised blessing! Jesus is the promised Seed of Abraham through whom all who receive Him are blessed with the Holy Spirit and become children of God, heirs of His Eternal Life of Sonship, in perfect righteousness, peace and joy with the Father.

The Holy Spirit is here to show you from the scriptures that there is no true Spirit of Apostleship possible outside of the righteousness that God revealed in Jesus when He brought Him into the world, in the body He prepared for Him, and declared Him to be His Son with power, according to the Spirit of holiness, by the resurrection from the dead. Only Jesus is the true Apostle of our God-given faith. It is therefore only through Jesus we are able to receive grace and Apostleship for obedience to the faith among all nations, among whom you also are called of Jesus Christ (Romans 1:3-6).

Selah.
Take a moment and worshipfully meditate on this and the Holy Spirit will refresh you in your union with the Father and the Son, who is Jesus Christ our Lord.

Chapter 4

THE SEED OF DAVID

God continues His great work - preparing a body for Jesus - even though He is surrounded by all that is contrary on earth to His Divine nature, character, and glory. You can see the greatness of God's power to fulfil His promise in the fourteen generations from Abraham to David, the fourteen generations from David to the time Israel went to Babylon, and the fourteen generations from Babylon to Jesus (Matthew 1:17).

God the Father demonstrates that He is love by sending His Son not to condemn the world but so the world through Him might be saved. This is why God says to the whole world and its leaders, in one of the most powerful of David's Psalms, "Why do the nations rage and the people plot a vain thing? The kings of the earth set themselves, and the rulers take counsel together, against the Lord and against His Anointed, saying, 'Let us break their bonds in pieces and cast away their cords from us.' He who sits in the heavens shall laugh; The Lord shall hold them in derision. Then He shall speak to them in His wrath and distress them in His deep displeasure: 'Yet I have set My King on My holy hill of Zion.' 'I will declare the decree the Lord has said to Me, 'You are My Son, today I have begotten You. Ask of Me, and I will give You the nations for Your inheritance, and the ends of the earth for Your possession. You shall break them with a rod of iron; You shall dash them to pieces like a potter's vessel.' Now therefore, be wise, O kings; be instructed, you judges of the earth. Serve the Lord with fear, and rejoice with trembling. Kiss the Son, lest He be angry, and you perish in the way, when His wrath is kindled but a little. Blessed are all those who put their trust in Him" (Psalm 2:1-12).

You see, Jesus is not only the Seed of Abraham, He is also the Seed of David. For God said, "I have found My servant David; with My holy oil I have anointed him, with whom My hand shall be established; also My arm shall strengthen him. The enemy shall not outwit him, nor the son of wickedness afflict him. I will beat down his foes before his face, and plague those who hate him. But My faithfulness and My mercy shall be with him, and in My name his horn shall be exalted. He shall cry to Me, 'You are my Father, My God, and the rock of my salvation.' Also, I will make him My firstborn" (Psalm 89:20-27). This David God raised up as King and Shepherd over His people, to whom also He gave testimony when He said, "David the son of Jesse is a man after My own heart, who will do all My will." From this man's seed, according to the promise, God raised up for Israel a Saviour - Jesus - who was born in Bethlehem, the city of David (Acts 13:22-23).

David's Prophetic Foresight

There is not enough room in this book to unfold all the wonders of God's handiwork in how He prepared a body for Jesus through David. For it is to David He says, "When your days are fulfilled and you rest with your fathers, I will set up your Seed after you, who will come from your body, and I will establish His kingdom. He shall build a house for My name, and I will establish the throne of His kingdom forever. I will be His Father, and He shall be My Son. And your house and your kingdom shall be established forever before you. Your throne shall be established forever" (2 Samuel 7:12-16).

David, being a prophet, knew that God had promised with an oath that one of his own descendants would sit on his throne as the Messiah - the Christ. God therefore let David see the future and showed him the resurrection of Jesus and how He would not leave Jesus among the dead, nor let His body decay in the grave, but would release Him from the horrors of death and raise Him, who is the Prince of Life, to reign upon His throne forever and ever.

It is so wonderful to see how the Spirit of Christ revealed in David what Jesus would go through in His suffering before the resurrection. David said, "I foresaw the Lord always before my face, for He is at my right hand, that I may not be shaken. Therefore, my heart rejoiced, and my tongue was glad; moreover, my flesh also will rest in hope. For You will not leave my soul in Hades, nor will You allow Your Holy One to see corruption. You have made known to me the ways of Life; You will make me full of joy in Your presence" (Psalm 16).

Think about this! David wasn't referring to himself when he spoke these words, for he died, and his body was buried and decayed. Nor did he ascend into the heaven to sit down at the right hand of God, but having the heart of God, he overheard the Father say, "The Lord said to my Lord, 'Sit at My right hand, till I make Your enemies Your footstool'." And, "The Lord has sworn and will not relent, 'You are a Priest forever according to the order of Melchizedek'" (Psalm 110).

Psalm 110 is the most frequently quoted Psalm of David in the New Testament. It helps you recognise that Jesus, who was crucified, died and rose again, is the One who is crowned with glory and honour, and is now seated at the right hand of the Majesty on high as both Lord and Christ, where He reigns as our great High Priest-King in the fullness of the blessed presence of the Father.

The Faith you see in Abraham is in David

As with Abraham, God revealed to David the unchangeable nature of His will when He promised that of his seed He would raise up for Israel a Saviour - Jesus - and confirmed His promise with an oath as it is written, "The Lord has sworn in truth to David; He will not turn from it: 'I will set upon your throne the fruit of your body'" (Psalm 132:11). This is why when David looked at his children, it was only through God's immense promise and oath that he, like Abraham, had hope against hope, that what God promised and sealed with an oath He Himself would perform. So that at the end of his natural life, David the son of Jesse said, "Thus says the man raised up on high, the anointed of the God of Jacob, and the sweet psalmist of Israel: The Spirit of the Lord spoke by me, His word was on my tongue. The Rock of Israel said to me: 'One shall come who rules righteously, who rules in the fear of God. He shall be as the light of the morning; a cloudless sunrise when the tender grass springs forth upon the earth; as sunshine after rain'." David said, "Although my house is not so with God, Yet He has made with me an everlasting covenant, ordered in all things and secure. For this is all my salvation and all my desire; will He not make it increase?" (2 Samuel 23:1-5).

Consider the greatness of God, that He enabled David to speak by His Spirit and declare that Jesus would be called the Son of David, be born of his seed, according to the flesh, and declared with power by the Holy Spirit to be the Son of God through the resurrection from the dead. Can you see the wonder and beauty of God's heart in David? How by His Spirit He enables him to call his own Son (Jesus) his Lord by saying: "The Lord said to my Lord, 'Sit at My right hand, till I make Your enemies Your footstool'." (Psalm 110; Matthew 22:41-45).

David, like Abraham, foresaw Jesus Christ becoming manifest in the body and spoke concerning His suffering, death, and resurrection, as well as the glory that would follow when He would ascend to heaven and sit at God's right hand.

All the glory belongs to God, the Father of our Lord Jesus Christ, whom He has made Jesus unto us. Jesus is not just any man, but according to His human body He is the promised Seed of the woman, the promised Seed of Abraham, and the promised Seed of David. The true Spirit of Apostleship has no other foundation that gives it such power and authority in heaven, on earth and under the earth than in Jesus alone, for Jesus who died and rose to Life is both Lord and Christ of the living and the dead (Romans 14:9).

Flooded with the Light of Christ's Life

I pray your tender heart is being flooded with the Light of Christ's Life as you read these words, so you can see the glory He is calling you to share with Him at the Father's right hand. Did you know that the heavenly Father has been made rich now that you belong to Him? And because of what Jesus has done for you, the Father is pleased to point to you as His beloved child by giving you the Holy Spirit. And did you know that the Holy Spirit rejoices to help you realise how mighty His power is to help you live as Jesus lives now that Jesus is your Life? The power by which you live as He lives is the same power by which Jesus rose from the dead and now reigns in glory. Just think about it - you have this precious treasure, this Light of Christ's Life and power in your weak human body, so that everyone can see that the glorious power by which you live is from God the Father and is not your own. You are truly a child of God, a new creation, for you now emanate the same Life we see in Jesus.

Remember, you have His Life-giving Spirit in you to reign with Him over every principality, power, might and dominion, and every name that is named. For God the Father has put all things under the feet of Jesus, and He and He alone is the supreme Head of the Church, which is His body, the fullness of Him who fills all in all, until we all become a body wholly filled and flooded with God Himself.

There are not enough words to describe the fullness of the Father's joy that you are now His child. I pray that your heart overflows with the joy of the Lord, for by His mighty power at work in you, Jesus is able to carry out God's purpose and conform you to His image, presenting you before the Father holy and without blame, well-pleasing in His sight. Jesus is able to do far more in and through you than you would ever dare ask - infinitely beyond your highest prayers, desires, thoughts, hopes or dreams.

Selah.
Take a moment and worshipfully meditate on this and the Holy Spirit will refresh you in your union with the Father and the Son, who is Jesus Christ our Lord.

Chapter 5

WHAT IS AN APOSTLE?

Jesus came forth from the bosom of the intimate presence of the Father to help us find and know the only true living God, for in all that Jesus is, says and does we see God. Jesus is therefore the perfect Spirit of Apostleship, not only in His nature as the only true living God, but also in the action of His perfect submission to obey and fulfil the will of the Father in all that is written of Him. For consider this, that after Jesus had fully cleared our record and removed every charge by His blood, He appeared to His disciples and said, "Peace to you. Why are you troubled? And why do doubts arise in your hearts? Behold My hands and My feet, that it is I Myself. Handle Me and see, for a spirit does not have flesh and bones as you see I have." He said, "These are the words which I spoke to you while I was still with you, that all things must be fulfilled which were written in the Law of Moses and the Prophets and the Psalms concerning Me." And He opened their understanding, that they might comprehend the Scriptures. Then He said to them, "Thus it is written, and thus it was necessary for the Christ to suffer and to rise from the dead the third day, and that repentance and remission of sins should be preached in His name to all nations, beginning at Jerusalem. And you are witnesses of these things. Behold, I send the Promise of My Father upon you; but tarry in the city of Jerusalem until you are endued with power from on high" (Luke 24:36-49).

Called, Chosen and Sent to represent Jesus

To understand what an Apostle is you need to know who Jesus is. Jesus' disciples saw the scriptures fulfilled in Jesus, they saw His Life in the Father and the Father in Him and thereby learned what it means to be an Apostle.

John begins his first letter by saying, "[we are writing] about the Word of Life [in] Him Who existed from the beginning, Whom we have heard, Whom we have seen with our [own] eyes, Whom we have gazed upon [for ourselves] and have touched with our [own] hands. And the Life [an aspect of His being] was revealed (made manifest, demonstrated), and we saw [as eyewitnesses] and are testifying to and declare to you the Life, the Eternal Life [in Him] Who already existed with the Father and Who [actually] was made visible (was revealed) to us [His followers]. What we have seen and [ourselves] heard, we are also telling you, so that you too may realize and enjoy fellowship as partners and partakers with us. And [this] fellowship that we have [which is a distinguishing mark of Christians] is with the Father and with His Son Jesus Christ (the Messiah)" (1 John 1:1-3 AMPC).

Can you now see what it means to be an Apostle?! Jesus speaking of Himself says, "There is another who bears witness of Me and I know that the witness which He witnesses of Me is true. The Father Himself, who sent Me has testified of Me. If you had known Me, you would have known My Father also; and from now on you know Him and have seen Him."

"He who has seen Me has seen the Father, so how can you say, show us the Father? Do you not believe that I am in the Father, and the Father in Me? The words that I speak to you I do not speak on My own authority; but the Father who dwells in Me does the works. Believe Me that I am in the Father and the Father in Me, or else believe Me for the sake of the works themselves."

"Most assuredly, I say to you, the Son can do nothing of Himself, but what He sees the Father do; for whatever

He does, the Son also does in like manner. For the Father loves the Son and shows Him all things that He Himself does; and He will show Him greater works than these, that you may marvel" (John 5:32-37, 14:7-14, 5:19-20).

Jesus is the true Spirit of Apostleship, for He perfectly embodies and represents the Father. Now with this in mind you now know what an Apostle looks like. Christ's Apostle is someone called, chosen, and sent by God the Father in whom He is pleased to reveal His Son, Jesus Christ the Lord. And by God's grace an Apostle is empowered by the Holy Spirit to open the scriptures and speak the Life-giving words of the new covenant, so that whoever believes in the name of Jesus Christ receives forgiveness of sins and Eternal Life in Him. Let me say this again so that it may deeply penetrate your heart: Christ's Apostle is someone in whom the Father is pleased to reveal His Son - so that in all this person is, says and does, Jesus is revealed in both word and deed, with signs and wonders, gifts of the Holy Spirit and various miracles.

Selah.
Take a moment and worshipfully meditate on this and the Holy Spirit will refresh you in your union with the Father and the Son, who is Jesus Christ our Lord.

Part 2
PETER, CHRIST'S APOSTLE

Chapter 6

CHRIST APPOINTED, NOT SELF-APPOINTED

Jesus prayed for His Apostles when He said, "Father I have told these men all about You. They were in the world, but then You gave them to Me. Actually, they were always Yours, and You gave them to Me; and they have kept Your word. Now they know that everything I have is a gift from You, for I have passed on to them the words You gave Me; and they accepted them and know that I came from You, and they believe You sent Me. O righteous Father, the world doesn't know You, but I do, and these disciples know You sent Me. For I have revealed You to them and will keep on revealing You so that the mighty love You have for Me may be in them, and I in them" (John 17:6-7, 26 TLB).

With this prayer in mind, consider how Peter became Christ's Apostle. The Father gave Peter to Jesus when He began to reveal in him that Jesus is the Christ, the Son of the living God. When Jesus saw this, He said to him, "You are blessed, Simon son of Jonah, because My Father in heaven has revealed this to you. You did not learn who I am from any human being. Now I say to you that you are Peter, and upon this rock (Jesus is the Rock) I will build My church, and all the powers of hell will not conquer it. And I will give you the keys of the kingdom of Heaven. Whatever you lock on earth will be locked in heaven, and whatever you open on earth will be open in heaven" (Matthew 16:16-20 NLT).

Peter had much to learn as Christ's Apostle, but the Father had given him to Jesus, Whose Life was being formed in him. This Life of Christ in Peter became the Rock on which God could build His house, which is the Church of the living God, the pillar and foundation of the truth (1 Timothy 3:15). While there are many things we can look at in Peter that identifies him as Christ's Apostle, what is fundamental and most essential for you to see is that the Father gave him to Jesus by revealing Jesus in him, which is also the reason why Jesus chose Peter to be His Apostle.

The Bread of Heaven

When Jesus began to unveil His Life with the Father as the bread of heaven and living water for Eternal Life, many left Jesus because their minds were spiritually blind. They could not see that Jesus is the fulfilment of the daily Manna given to Israel in the wilderness, as well as the Rock that followed them, from which the water flowed. These things were but a shadow of the good things to come in Jesus. However, God was pleased to show His glory to Israel in the wilderness. But what their eyes could not see, their ears could not hear, nor their hearts perceive, is now revealed by the Holy Spirit in Jesus. Their experience of God's provision of daily bread, as well as water from the Rock, shows us what God now freely gives by His Spirit in Jesus.

Israel had to learn to trust God to provide their daily bread and believe Him that the Rock would never fail to quench their thirst; and we have their example to learn to live by faith in Jesus and know that we have Eternal Life in Him. Just as the bread and water gave nourishment for living in the wilderness, so Jesus renews us inwardly, day by day, continually and forever by the Holy Spirit, so that we may live on earth as He lives in heaven.

Jesus is the Bread God gives from heaven. All who receive Him will never hunger or lack anything for life and godliness while living in this world. Jesus said, "As the living

Father sent Me, and I live because of the Father, so he who feeds on Me will live because of Me" (John 6:57). Jesus is the Rock from Whom the Life-giving water flows, so that all who believe in Him will never thirst but have a continual supply of the Holy Spirit to live as He lives - in unbroken, perfect oneness and fellowship with the Father.

Many left Jesus when they heard Him teach this glorious truth of the new covenant, that they would receive Eternal Life by feeding on Him. When that happened, Jesus asked the few remaining disciples if they wanted to leave Him too. Peter replied, "Lord, to whom shall we go? You have the words of Eternal Life. Also, we have come to believe and know that You are the Christ, the Son of the living God." When Jesus heard Peter say this He said, "Did I not choose you?" (John 6:68-70).

Can you see why Jesus chose Peter? It was because Jesus could see that the Father revealed who He is in Peter. Fundamentally, this is what made Peter Christ's Apostle!

Satan opposes God

Right from the beginning there was a conflict with satan over Peter becoming Christ's Apostle. I say this to encourage you to trust Jesus, for He will see you through every battle in life and will never fail to make you all you are called to be in Him.

The word "satan" means "adversary" or "accuser." This highlights the fact that satan opposes God's will in our lives. The conflict he causes is plainly described in scripture. You can see him oppose God when He bore a favourable witness concerning His servant Job. God said, "Have you considered My servant Job, that there is none like him on the earth, a blameless and upright man, one who fears God and shuns evil?" (Job 1:8).

In Job's life you see how satan came against God by causing all the suffering Job experienced. He did this to try to disprove what God said about him, that he was blameless, and to prove that Job's love for Him was worthless. But God believed in Job and that whatever satan did to him, Job's faith and love would not fail.

I love Job because when he suffered, he worshipped God instead of blaming Him. What Job believed and said about God set him apart. Job said, "I know that my Redeemer lives. He knows what I am like. While His breath is in me, I will never give up being right in His sight. I will not let my own heart reproach me, for I know that when He has finished searching my heart, He Himself will bring me forth, pure as gold. There is nothing He cannot do, and no purpose can be withheld from Him" (Job 19:25, 27:3-6, 23:10, 42:2).

See how God's Word concerning Job prevailed when God made a spectacle of satan before heaven and earth and completely disarmed him, when He lifted Job's face in His presence. You see even while Job was still suffering, God granted him the priceless High Priestly privilege to minister forgiveness on His behalf to the men who had misrepresented Him, when they persecuted Job with the claim that the root cause of all his afflictions was found in him (Job 19:28 AMP). When Job prayed and ministered God's forgiveness, he was restored and was given more than ever before. In heaven he has no small reward, as he is acknowledged next to Noah and Daniel (Ezekiel 14:14,20).

When I look at Job, I see Jesus our great High Priest on the cross, Who in His suffering, when justice was denied Him, made intercession for us; and by His own Holy blameless blood, disarmed satan as He took away his power to accuse us. Jesus made a spectacle of satan as He triumphed over him when He, in His amazing grace, fully cleared our record and removed every charge and judgment against us, freely forgiving all our sins.

You can also see how satan opposed God when he sought to undermine His Word in Jesus. Remember when Jesus was baptised, He prayed and the heavens opened, the Holy Spirit was seen descending and remaining upon Him, and the Father was heard saying to Him, "You are My Beloved Son; in You I am well pleased." Immediately, while being led by the Holy Spirit, satan came to tempt Jesus by seeking to sow his evil thoughts into His heart saying, "If You are the Son of God, why don't You...." but Jesus, being full of the Holy Spirit and power, withstood satan by saying, "It is written, 'Man shall not live by bread alone, but by every Word of God'" (Luke 3:21-22, 4:4; Deuteronomy 8:3).

Satan opposes God concerning Peter

Now consider how satan opposed God concerning Peter. For from the moment the Father revealed in him that Jesus is the Christ, the Son of the Living God and Jesus began to share why the Father sent Him, Peter was caught in the crossfire of satan's opposition to Jesus doing the Father's will. You can see how Peter was not yet able to recognise and withstand satan's opposing thoughts, as he began to express them by rebuking Jesus. However, Jesus refused to let satan get a grip on Peter when He turned and said, "Get behind Me, Satan! You are an offense, a hindrance to Me, for you are not mindful of the things of God, you are seeing things merely from a human point of view, not from God's" (Matthew 16:23).

It took time for Peter and the other disciples to have the mind of Christ and learn from Him how to withstand satan. Even on the night before His death when Jesus shared how one of them would betray Him, and while they discussed who could do such a thing, the conversation turned into a dispute about who was the greatest among them. Jesus responded by showing them that their thoughts were not from the Father but from the world. He said, "those who exercise authority in this world by using their wealth are called 'benefactors', and those who rule are considered great and are even deified as they lord it over you. But it shall not be so among you. Look at Me, I am One among you who serves" (Luke 22:25-27).

Then Jesus said to Peter, who was like the first among them, "Simon, Simon (Peter), listen! Satan has asked excessively that [all of] you be given up to him [out of the power and keeping of God], that he might sift [all of] you like grain, [Job 1:6-12; Amos 9:9.] But I have prayed especially for you [Peter], that your [own] faith may not fail; and when you yourself have turned again, strengthen and establish your brethren" (Luke 22:31-32 AMPC).

I love seeing the Father's love in Jesus, revealed through His faith for Peter. For even while satan sought to trouble Peter to prove he was worthless like chaff, Jesus prayed for Peter to prove that his faith was the true grain of God's Word living in his heart and that his faith would not fail.

Here you can see what Jesus prayed, "I am no more in the world, but these are [still] in the world, and I am coming to You. Holy Father keep in Your Name [in the knowledge of Yourself] those whom You have given Me, that they may be one as We [are one]. I do not ask that You will take them out of the world, but that You will keep and protect them from the evil one" (John 17:11,15 AMPC).

Jesus shows through His prayers for Peter that the faith He knew the Father had given him was not worthless but precious, and that Peter, through faith, would overcome satan's temptations. Jesus knew Peter would humble himself in heartfelt repentance, return to Him and fully recover and grow strong as His Apostle to strengthen others.

Peter learned through his union with Jesus how to resist satan by staying in faith! You can see how Peter strengthened and establish the brethren, in fulfilment of Jesus' prayer, when he says: "Be sober-minded; be watchful. Your adversary the devil prowls around like a roaring lion, seeking someone to devour. Resist him, firm in your faith, knowing that the same kinds of suffering are being experienced by your brotherhood throughout the world. And after you have suffered a little while, the God of all grace, who has called you to His eternal glory in Christ, will himself restore, confirm, strengthen, and establish you. To him be the dominion forever and ever. Amen" (1 Peter 5:8-11 ESV).

Acknowledged by Jesus as His Apostle

There are many things we can learn in how God made Peter Christ's Apostle, but what is evident in God making Peter, is that the faith He had given him is the faith that overcomes the world. Jesus recognised the Father as the One who gave Peter this faith, so when He prayed for Peter, Jesus was working with the Father.

One thing I love about Christ's Apostles is the knowledge the Father gives them of His Son. This knowledge of who Jesus is comes from the Father and is the only power given unto man by which he can triumph over the spirit of the anti-Christ in this world. Jesus said, "No one knows the Son except the Father!" This is also why the Holy Spirit Who proceeds from the Father, and Who is the Spirit of Truth, testifies, declares and reveals Jesus in you (Matthew 11:27; John 15:26).

It is essential you learn from Jesus how He acknowledged those whom the Father gave Him to be His Apostles. For an

Apostle is not self-appointed. This is the work of the Father, as it is written, for not he who commends himself is approved, but whom the Lord commends (2 Corinthians 10:18). Peter became Christ's Apostle when Jesus saw the Father reveal Him in Peter; for Jesus is the Rock in Peter through whom the Holy Spirit would flow so powerfully on the day of Pentecost. As Jesus said, "You will know that I am in My Father, and you in Me, and I in you" (John 14:20).

Selah.
Take a moment and worshipfully meditate on this and the Holy Spirit will refresh you in your union with the Father and the Son, who is Jesus Christ our Lord.

Chapter 7

THE WORD AND THE SPIRIT

When the day of Pentecost had fully come, and the Holy Spirit was being poured out, Peter stood up and spoke as the Spirit gave him utterance. Now consider how masterfully he opened the scriptures to show what was written by the prophet Joel: "'And it shall come to pass in the last days', says God, 'that I will pour out of My Spirit on all flesh... And whoever calls on the name of the Lord shall be saved.'" It is very important that you see how the Holy Spirit enabled Peter to speak God's Word and thereby open the people's understanding, that they might comprehend the scriptures. For in Jesus all God's promises are yes so that we may say amen to the glory of God (2 Corinthians 1:20).

Remember how Peter saw the glory of God in Jesus on the mount of transfiguration, when "the appearance of His face was altered and His robe became white and glistening. And two men talked with Him, who were Moses and Elijah, who appeared in glory and spoke of His death which He was about to accomplish at Jerusalem. A bright cloud overshadowed them; and a voice came out of the cloud, saying, "This is My Beloved Son, in whom I am well pleased. Hear Him!"" (Luke 9:28-26).

What I want you to see is how through Jesus the scriptures are opened up to us. Peter says, "We heard this voice which came from heaven when we were with Him on the holy mountain. And so, we have the prophetic word confirmed, which you do well to heed as a light that shines in a dark place, until the day dawns and the morning star rises in your hearts; knowing this first, that no prophecy of Scripture is of any private interpretation, for prophecy never came by the will of man, but holy men of God spoke as they were moved by the Holy Spirit" (2 Peter 1:18-21).

Peter said the prophets prophesied about the salvation God prepared for us in Jesus, and they had many questions as to what it all could mean. They wondered what the Spirit of Christ within them was talking about when He told them in advance about Christ's suffering and His great glory afterwards. They wondered when and to whom all this would happen. They were told that these things would not happen during their lifetime, but many years later, during ours. And now this Good News about which they prophesied is being announced by those who preach to you in the power of the Holy Spirit sent from heaven. This is all so wonderful that even the angels are eagerly watching these things happen (1 Peter 1:10-12 TLB).

Hereby you can see that the work of God in an Apostle is to give him power to open the scriptures and unveil the ever-living Word, which is none other than Jesus Christ Himself. Jesus is the Word who became flesh and dwelt among us (John 1:14).

Let me say this again, so that it may deeply penetrate your heart: Christ's Apostles are those to whom it is given to open the scriptures to give the faith that Jesus is the Christ. For the substance, the essence of the Truth is revealed in and by Jesus - He is the Spirit of all prophecy. In other words, the purpose of all prophecy is to tell about Jesus. He is and must be the vital breath, the inspiration of all inspired preaching and interpretation of God's divine will and purpose (Revelation 19:10 AMP).

Christ's Apostle opens the Scriptures

You can see Peter is Christ's Apostle in that gospel he preached by the power of the heaven-sent Holy Spirit was not made up of his own ideas. Through Jesus, the writings of the Prophets became alive, active and sharper than any two-edged sword, piercing even to the division of soul and spirit, and of joints and marrow, for the Word of God is a discerner of the thoughts and intents of the heart. There is no creature hidden from God's sight, but all things are naked and open to the eyes of Him to whom we must give account (Hebrews 4:12-13).

Peter said, "Men of Israel, hear these words: Jesus of Nazareth, a Man attested by God to you by miracles, wonders, and signs which God did through Him in your midst, as you yourselves also know - Him, being delivered by the determined purpose and foreknowledge of God, you have taken by lawless hands, have crucified, and put to death; whom God raised up, having loosed the pains of death, because it was not possible that He should be held by it. For David says concerning Him: 'I foresaw the Lord always before my face, for He is at my right hand, that I may not be shaken. Therefore, my heart rejoiced, and my tongue was glad; moreover my flesh also will rest in hope. For You will not leave my soul in Hades, nor will You allow Your Holy One to see corruption. You have made known to me the ways of life, You will make me full of joy in Your presence'."

Peter says, "Men and brethren, let me speak freely to you of the patriarch David that he is both dead and buried, and his tomb is with us to this day. Therefore, being a prophet, and knowing that God had sworn with an oath to him that of the fruit of his body, according to the flesh, He would raise up the Christ to sit on his throne, he, foreseeing this, spoke concerning the resurrection of the Christ, that His soul was not left in Hades, nor did His flesh see corruption. This Jesus God has raised up of which we are all witnesses. Therefore, being exalted to the right hand of God, and having received from the Father the promise of the Holy

Spirit, He poured out this which you now see and hear. For David did not ascend into the heavens, but he says himself: 'The Lord said to my Lord, "Sit at My right hand, till I make Your enemies Your footstool"'. Therefore, let all the house of Israel know assuredly that God has made this Jesus, whom you crucified, both Lord and Christ."

"Now when they heard this, they were cut to the heart, and said to Peter and the rest of the Apostles, 'Men and brethren, what shall we do?' Then Peter said to them, 'Repent, and let every one of you be baptized in the name of Jesus Christ for the remission of sins; and you shall receive the gift of the Holy Spirit. For the promise is to you and to your children, and to all who are afar off, as many as the Lord our God will call'" (Acts 2:29-39).

Can you see how God worked mightily through Peter to open the scriptures to give the faith that Jesus is the Christ, the Son of the Living God, in a most hostile political and religious environment?

The Word and the Works of God

The work of God is not only seen in the way He opens His Word through Peter, but also in the way He performs His works through Peter. I say this so that you may know that Christ's Apostle is someone of both the Word and the Spirit. Someone who knows both the Scriptures and the power of God.

Remember, Jesus said, "The works which the Father has given Me to finish - the very works that I do - bear witness of Me, that the Father has sent Me. The words that I speak to you I do not speak on My own authority; but the Father who dwells in Me does the works. Believe Me that I am in the Father and the Father in Me, or else believe Me for the sake of the works themselves" (John 5:36, 14:10-11). Jesus also said, "This is the work of God; that you believe in Him whom He sent" (John 6:29).

When Jesus spoke about the work of God, He spoke in a language all Christ's Apostles must learn. Jesus spoke in Oneness with the Father. He said, "If you had known Me, you would have known My Father also; and from now on you know Him and have seen Him. He who has seen Me has seen the Father. You believe in God believe also in Me, for he who believes in Me, the works that I do he will do also; and greater works than these he will do, because I go to My Father. And whatever you ask the Father representing Me, in My name, that I will do, that the Father may be glorified in the Son. If you ask the Father anything representing Me, in My name, I will do it" (John 14:7-14).

When Jesus talked about doing the work of God, all He could see was the Father in Him doing the works, so that all who heard His voice believed in Him as they believe in the Father. What the Holy Spirit is showing you here is that Jesus unveiled in Himself not only who the Father is but also the works He now gives to His Apostles. For Christ's Apostle, to do the work of God is more important than you may realise, for the works an Apostle does bear witness of him that he represents Jesus and is sent by Him.

Recognising the Father in Jesus

You see an Apostle is an Apostle because he represents and presents Jesus and not himself. An Apostle is an Apostle because the Father works with him, drawing everyone to Jesus, so that through Jesus they may receive a warm welcome in His presence (2 Corinthians 6:1-2 TLB). Therefore, the fundamental power and authority of Christ's Apostle is the Father working with him bearing witness of His Son in word and deed with signs and wonders, various miracles, and gifts of the Holy Spirit, according to His own will (Hebrews 2:4). For whoever acknowledges the Son has the Father also (1 John 2:23).

Jesus clearly shows what this means when He spoke to those who thought they knew God because they had a form of godliness, but did not realise that they did not know Him for they denied Him by refusing to recognise and receive Him in Jesus. Jesus said, "The Father Himself, who sent Me, has testified of Me, however you have neither heard His voice at any time, nor seen His form. You do not have His word abiding in you, because whom He sent, Him you do not believe. You search the Scriptures, for in them you think you have Eternal Life but these are they which testify of Me. But you are not willing to come to Me that you may have Life."

"I do not receive honour from men. But I know you, that you do not have the love of God in you; because I have come in My Father's name, representing and revealing Him and His presence, and you do not receive Me; if another comes in his own name, representing only himself, him you will receive. How can you believe I have come from My Father and represent Him, when you rather receive honour from one another, and do not seek the honour that comes from the only God? Do not think that I shall accuse you to the Father; there is one who accuses you - Moses, in whom you trust. For if you believed Moses, you would believe Me; for he wrote about Me. But if you do not believe his writings, how will you believe My words?" (John 5:37-46).

What Jesus was saying to those who would not receive Him is: "How can you say you know God whom you cannot see, when He is in Me whom you can see? You who search the scriptures, for in them you think you have Eternal Life, do not realise that these are they which testify of Me, yet Me you will not receive that you may have Life. If the scriptures were truly living in you then you would recognise that I have come from My Father, and if His love were in you, you would receive Me."

The work of God is to Believe in Jesus

What I would like you to see is that the work of God in Jesus is the same work you see in Peter. Peter shows that he knows God because he believed the witness God gave of His Son, Jesus. Remember how the Father revealed Jesus in Peter when he said, "You are the Christ, the Son of the Living God." Now, this is what it means to be Christ's Apostle, for this is the work of God, that you may believe in Him, know Him and receive Him in Jesus. And this is also the purpose for which He opens the scriptures to you and in you, so that through them you may believe and recognise that Jesus is the Christ, the Son of the living God.

When Peter preached the Gospel he said, "We have not been telling you fairy tales when we explained to you the power of our Lord Jesus Christ and His coming again. My own eyes have seen His splendour and His glory: I was there on the holy mountain when He shone out with honour given Him by God His Father; I heard that glorious, majestic voice calling down from heaven, saying, 'This is My much-loved Son; I am well pleased with Him.' So, we have seen and proved that what the prophets said came true. You will do well to pay close attention to everything they have written, for, like lights shining into dark corners, their words help us to understand many things that otherwise would be dark and difficult. But when you consider the wonderful truth of the prophets' words, then the Light will dawn in your souls and Christ the Morning Star will shine in your hearts. For no prophecy recorded in Scripture was ever thought up by the prophet himself. It was the Holy Spirit within these godly men who gave them true messages from God" (2 Peter 1:16-20 TLB).

In Peter, you can clearly see how Christ's Apostle, anointed with the Holy Spirit and power, will triumph in any place or time - over the world, the anti-Christ and all the powers of darkness. For while Peter was persecuted, an angel of God led him out of prison and said to him, "Go, stand in the temple and speak to the people all the words of this Life" (Acts 5:20).

I cannot emphasise enough the work of God you see in Peter - how the Holy Spirit enabled him to open the scriptures and speak the words of this Life by revealing that Jesus is the Christ, the Son of the living God. Peter shows by the power of the Holy Spirit that Jesus is the incorruptible, ever-living Word of God. His Apostolic authority and power to speak the Word of God are proof that God was working in him and with him. For when he spoke, as many as received the words he spoke were born again - made alive with Jesus and filled with the Holy Spirit.

Ten years after the day of Pentecost, when Peter was in Joppa, he was full of the Holy Spirit and power having just raised Dorcas from the dead. Jesus then sent him to Cornelius' house in Caesarea. "While Peter was still speaking about how God anointed Jesus of Nazareth with the Holy Spirit and with power, who went about doing good and healing all who were oppressed by the devil, for God was with Him - the Holy Spirit fell upon all those who heard the words Peter spoke. And those of the circumcision who believed were astonished, as many as came with Peter, because the gift of the Holy Spirit had been poured out on the Gentiles also. For they heard them speak with tongues and magnify God. Then Peter answered, 'Can anyone forbid water, that these should not be baptized who have received the Holy Spirit just as we have?'" (Acts 10:38, 44-47).

What is so important for you to see is how God worked with Peter confirming His Word. Peter said, "This Jesus, Whom God has raised up, of which we are all witnesses. He is exalted to the right hand of God and having received from the Father the promise of the Holy Spirit, He poured out this which you now see and hear" (Acts 2:33).

Drawing near to the Father

I say all of this because before Jesus was glorified the Holy Spirit points out, through the veil in the temple, that the way into the true Holy of Holies - God's blessed presence - was not yet open, disclosed or manifest. Only the high priest could enter beyond the veil, into what was but a copy of the Holy of Holies, once a year with the blood of atonement which he sprinkled on the mercy seat. God provided this example to show what we now receive through Jesus. You see, Jesus' body, representing the true veil, was torn when He shed His blood and died at Calvary. The moment He died, the veil in the temple was torn from top to bottom, whereby the Holy Spirit signifies that Jesus has opened the new Life-giving Way through the veil, that is His body, into the true Holy of Holiest where He ever lives to make intercession, to give us a warm welcome in the presence of the Father. Jesus gives perfect freedom and confidence to enter the true Holy of Holies because He cleanses our hearts with His blood from consciousness of sin and baptises us with the Holy Spirit. Nothing can stop us from drawing near to the Father for we have been made perfectly accepted in the beloved, Jesus, Who continually fills us with the Holy Spirit. Jesus is the Way for us all to draw near to the Father, by One Spirit and enjoy perfect fellowship with Him (Matthew 27:51; Hebrews 9:8, 10:10-22; Ephesians 2:18).

I pray you can hear and see the Apostolic, new covenant Gospel in Peter, for all who heard him speak about Jesus and believed, received the Holy Spirit whom Jesus gives - the Spirit of Truth who proceeds from the Father. Through the Gospel Peter preached, it is clear to see that we are now living in the new covenant, for we have the Holy Spirit's blessed presence within us as God's guarantee that we really are His children, that we share in the inheritance of the saints in the Light and are members of His household. Our greatest joy is to draw near to the Father, or should I say, our greatest joy is that the Father is drawing us near to Himself by His Spirit, now that He has made us Holy, acceptable and well-pleasing in His sight through Jesus Christ.

To the Glory of God Alone

When Peter and John were about to go into the temple to pray, they saw a lame man begging at the gate. Peter said, "Look at us," as he took him by the hand and said, "In the name of Jesus Christ of Nazareth, rise up and walk. Immediately the man's feet and ankle bones received strength, so he leaped up and entered the temple with them while praising God."

This so amazed everyone, as the healed man held on to Peter, that Peter said to them: "Why do you marvel at this? Or look at us as though by our own power or godliness we made this man walk. God, the God of our father Abraham, Isaac, and Jacob, glorified His Servant Jesus, the Prince of Life, whom He raised from the dead, of which we are witnesses. And His name, through faith in His name, has made this man strong, whom you see and know. Yes, the faith which comes through Him has given him this perfect soundness in the presence of you all" (Acts 3). Peter knew the power by which he raised this man was not his own but came through faith in Jesus' name.

As Christ's Apostle, Peter had no thought to promote himself. As a representative of Jesus, he bore witness by the power of the Holy Spirit that Jesus is raised from the dead, living at God's right hand, so that all who heard the words he spoke would come to believe that Jesus is the Christ, the Son of the living God. As a fisherman Peter was considered unlearned and uneducated, but as Christ's Apostle everyone could see that the same Life of God that emanated from Jesus was in him. What joy it is to see the Father working with Peter, confirming the words he spoke with accompanying signs and wonders - healing this lame man.

This is a distinguishing characteristic in all Christ's Apostles - they always contend for God to be glorified through His Son. Peter said, "All the honour belongs to God the Father of our Lord Jesus Christ who in His boundless mercy has given us the privilege to be born again and become members of His family. And because He raised Jesus from the dead, God has given us hope for Eternal Life in Him" (1 Peter 1:3-4). Jesus who is our Life; He is our ever-living hope, He is the anchor for our soul, He is our blessed assurance and foretaste of glory divine.

So you can clearly see that Peter is Christ's Apostle for he lived in the revelation that Jesus is our Life and that He is kept perfectly pure and undefiled, beyond the reach of change and decay at God's right hand. You can also see that it was God's will to approve Peter as Christ's Apostle by this unfading Life that flowed unhindered from him by the power of the Holy Spirit when he spoke about Jesus.

Selah.
Take a moment and worshipfully meditate on this and the Holy Spirit will refresh you in your union with the Father and the Son, who is Jesus Christ our Lord.

Chapter 8

PREACHING AND PROTECTING THE GOSPEL

What stands out in the Gospel that all Christ's Apostles preached is that Jesus is the ever-living hope of Eternal Life and that He is coming again!

For Peter, the Gospel was always relevant for everyone. He said, "Repent therefore and be converted, that your sins may be blotted out, so that times of refreshing may come from the presence of the Lord, and that He may send Jesus Christ, who was preached to you before, whom heaven must receive until the times of restoration of all things, which God has spoken by the mouth of all His holy prophets since the world began" (Acts 3:19-21).

You can see that the message of the Gospel does not change over time because years later, in his first letter, Peter continues the same message - Christ is coming back and we must endure all things by faith, living holy lives, as we wait for His return. He writes, "You are now being kept by the power of God through faith for salvation ready to be revealed in the last time. In this you greatly rejoice, though now for a little while, if need be, you have been grieved by various trials, that the genuineness of your faith, being much more precious than gold that perishes, though it is tested by fire, may be found to praise, honour, and glory at the revelation of Jesus Christ, whom having not seen, you love. Though now you do not see Him, yet believing, you rejoice with joy inexpressible and full of glory, receiving the end of your faith - the salvation of your souls.

Therefore gird up the loins of your mind, be sober, and rest your hope fully upon the grace that is to be brought to you at the revelation of Jesus Christ; as obedient children, not conforming yourselves to the former lusts, as in your ignorance, but as He who called you is holy, you also be holy in all your conduct, because it is written, 'Be holy, for I am holy'." (1 Peter 1:5-16).

The faith that the Apostles gave through the Gospel they preached prepared a Holy Spirit-filled people for God - people whose hope is the joy that will be revealed at the appearing of Jesus.

Beware of False Teaching

Christ's Apostles preached the good news of a born again, transformed, Holy Spirit-filled, sinless Life through faith in Jesus Christ. Not only that, but they stood against those who sought to preach what was not real in themselves, those who did not know Christ inwardly, those who were not sent by God, those who did not represent Jesus Christ - who did not have His Life-giving Spirit in them and deceived people with empty promises and lifeless words that had no transforming power.

Jesus warned us all, "Beware of false prophets/teachers, who come to you in sheep's clothing, but inwardly they are ravenous wolves. You will know them by their fruits" (Matthew 7:15-16). All Christ's Apostles warned God's people not to be naive about who they would receive but to pursue the love of the Way, the Truth and the Life that is found in Jesus Christ alone. Through His Life Jesus renews us inwardly daily so that we may live as He lives in perfect fellowship with the Father.

Peter shows that while the godly suffer temptations and trials in this world, the Lord Jesus - who bears long with their weaknesses - knows how, by His grace and power, to deliver them and make them what they ought to be - established, grounded and securely settled and strengthened in Him. Peter shares how that grace and peace - which is perfect wellbeing, all necessary good, all spiritual prosperity, and freedom from fears, agitating passions and moral conflicts - are multiplied to us in the full, personal, precise, and correct knowledge of God the Father and of Jesus Christ our Lord. At the same time, he warns that the ungodly are kept under chastisement until the day of judgment and doom.

It is of deep concern that an ungodly generation shrugs its shoulders at the reverential fear of God and mocks His judgement against sin by the way they live. Peter warns the Church of such ungodly behaviour by saying that God did not even spare the angels who sinned, but threw them into hell, chained in gloomy caves and darkness until judgment day. And He did not spare any of the people who lived in ancient times before the flood except Noah, a preacher of righteousness, who spoke up for God. Only he and his family of seven were saved. At that time God cleansed the whole world of ungodly men when He brought the flood upon them (Genesis 6-8; 1 Peter 3:20). And later, after He had delivered Lot - whose righteous soul was afflicted day by day living among the people of Sodom and Gomorrah, seeing and hearing their sins - He rained fire down upon those cities and turned them into heaps of ashes and blotted them off the face of the earth, making them an example for all the ungodly in the future, like in our days, to look back upon and fear.

God's Judgment Against Sin

It is very important that we do not disregard the warnings of Christ's Apostles about those who have let go of the cross of

Christ and His power to triumph over the sin-nature and have given themselves over to satisfy the lust of their flesh by indulging in polluting passions of immorality and greed. Of what value is the great sacrifice Jesus has made for us, if we deliberately keep sinning against Him, even though we have received the knowledge of the truth that Jesus subdued, overcame and deprived sin of its power over all who accept that sacrifice. It is as if we do not care about the sacrifice He made for us. It is vital Christ's Apostles let everyone know that there is not, and never will be, any other sacrifice for sin, so that if anyone rejects what Jesus has done for them there is nothing left except a terrible expectation of being condemned to the fire that will burn up God's enemies.

Peter says that it is important we understand what will happen in the last days in which we are living. He says that people will laugh at you and think it is strange that you do not live in sexual sins, evil desires, drunkenness and wild drinking parties like they do, so they insult you, because they love doing the evil things they want to do (1 Peter 4:3-4). They say, "Jesus promised to come again. Where is He? Our fathers have died, but the world continues the way it has been since it was made." But they do not want to remember what happened long ago. By the Word of God, He made the heavens and earth and brought the earth out from the water and surrounded it with water. Then the world was flooded and destroyed with water. And that same Word of God is keeping heaven and earth in order for it to be destroyed by fire. These people who insist on being ungodly are being kept for the Judgment Day and the destruction of all who are against God. Do not forget this one thing: to the Lord one day is as a thousand years, and a thousand years is as one day. The Lord is not slow in doing what He promised - the way some people understand slowness. But God is being patient for He does not want anyone to be lost, but He wants all people to come to repentance and live the Life He gives through Jesus. The Day of the Lord's judgment will come like a thief in the night. The skies will disappear with a loud noise. Everything in them will be destroyed by fire and the earth and everything in it will be burned up.

So what kind of people should we be? We should live holy lives and serve God as we wait for and look forward to that coming Day, for God has made a promise to us of a new heaven and a new earth in which righteousness, freedom from sin, and right standing with God shall abide (Isaiah 65:17, 66:22). From the garden of Eden where Adam and Eve sinned until now, God has clearly shown His judgment against sin. Peter reminds us that when anyone rejected the Law God gave through Moses, they died without mercy when only two or three testified against them. And in the Book of Hebrews we learn that if this was the punishment under the old covenant, how much greater the punishment a person deserves if he tramples underfoot God's Own Son, treating the sacrifice of His blood as of no account by being unremorseful, refusing to repent by continuing to sin when he knows that the sacrifice of Jesus' blood is what makes him holy before God. Such a person insults the Holy Spirit by throwing God's grace back into His face.

We should never forget that God has said, "Vengeance is Mine [retribution and the meting out of full justice rest with Me]; I will repay [I will exact the compensation], says the Lord. And again, The Lord will judge and determine and solve and settle the cause and the cases of His people" (Deuteronomy 32:35,36). "It is a fearful (formidable and terrible) thing to incur the divine penalties and be cast into the hands of the living God!" (Hebrews 10:31).

The Rise of False Teachers

Peter is speaking to the Church when he warns against false teachers who secretly teach things that are wrong; the kind of teaching that will cause people to be lost because it encourages them to continue in their sins. These teachers, in their hearts and their ways, have refused to accept Jesus, who bought their freedom, and Peter says that they will suffer a swift and terrible end. Many who follow their evil teaching think there is nothing wrong with sexual sin and greed. Peter shows that these teachers have an un-regenerated heart and mind and do not live daily crucified with Christ; for no woman can escape their sinful stare, and of adultery and lust they never have enough. They even make a game of luring unstable women. Peter says these teachers "do whatever they feel like and are a disgrace and a stain among you, deceiving you by living in foul sin on the side while they join you as though they were honest men. And because of them Christ and His way is scoffed at."

Peter also says, "These teachers in their greed will tell you anything to get hold of your money. They train themselves to be greedy; and are doomed and cursed. They have gone off the road and become lost like Balaam, the son of Be-or who had been given a gift to know things by the Spirit of God, so much so that he even prophesied about the coming of Jesus Christ saying, 'I see Him, but not now; I behold Him, but not near; A Star shall come out of Jacob; A Sceptre shall rise out of Israel'" (Numbers 24:17).

While Balaam was blessed with such a wonderful gift, he fell in love with the money he could make by doing wrong, and seduced God's people with immorality and an interest to worship other things. He was stopped from his mad course when his donkey spoke to him with a human voice, scolding and rebuking him. Sadly, later he and his household were destroyed along with the ungodly (Revelation 2:14; Numbers 31:8-16).

Peter continues his urgent plea to guard against false teachers by saying they are "as useless as dried-up springs of water or as clouds blown away by the wind - promising much and delivering nothing. They are doomed to blackest darkness. They brag about themselves with empty, foolish boasting. With lustful desire as their bait, they lure back into sin those who have just escaped from such wicked living. They promise freedom, but they themselves are slaves to sin and corruption, for a man is a slave to whatever controls him."

I pray that you can see the reason and the need for such a fervent warning from Peter; when the people who have escaped from the wicked ways of the world by learning about our Lord and Saviour Jesus Christ, then get tangled up with sin and become its slave again. They are then worse off than before. Peter says it would have been better if they had never known the right way to live than to know it and then reject the holy commandments that were given to them. They make these proverbs come true: "A dog returns to its vomit," and, "A washed pig returns to the mud" (2 Peter 2:22 AMP/TLB).

Clean in God's Eyes

I know what I have shared with you can be misunderstood by those who say they know Jesus but do not express His self-sacrificial love and power for those who need Him to help them overcome temptation and learn how to live free from the awful nature of sin. But I trust that as you have read Peter's urgent, strong and poignant warnings, you will remember how Jesus "Himself [in His humanity] has suffered in being tempted (tested and tried). And that He is able [immediately] to run to the cry of (assist, relieve) those who are being tempted and tested and tried [and who therefore are being exposed to suffering]". For you know that we do not have a High Priest Who is unable to understand and sympathise and have a shared feeling with our weaknesses and infirmities and liability to the assaults of temptation, but One Who has been tempted in every respect as we are, yet without sinning.

Therefore your life and ministry must always encourage everyone to "fearlessly and confidently and boldly draw near to the throne of grace (the throne of God's unmerited favour to us sinners), that we may receive mercy [for our failures] and find grace to help in good time for every need [appropriate help and well-timed help, coming just when we need it]" (Hebrews 2:18, 4:15-16 AMP/AMPC).

It is very important to remember that no true Apostle is exempt from the responsibility of establishing the Church of Jesus Christ firmly on the only true foundation that overcomes sin, triumphs over temptation and provides such glorious freedom from the fear of the judgment to come - the price Jesus paid for our sins on the cross in His own precious blood, through His death, His resurrection and glory at the Father's right hand, where He ever lives to make intercession and to give the Holy Spirit and every blessing of His Life with the Father.

The Church must never fail to be the witness and embodiment of Jesus Christ and His all-powerful, transforming, holy, sinless everlasting Life! The Church has the power to preach the gospel by the heaven-sent Holy Spirit and offer so great a salvation to all nations, tongues, tribes and people, to the glory of God. The Church must always be like a mighty, Holy Spirit-filled washing machine! You cannot be a part of it without being washed, made new, Spiritually alive, and clean in God's eyes.

Selah.
Take a moment and worshipfully meditate on this and the Holy Spirit will refresh you in your union with the Father and the Son, who is Jesus Christ our Lord.

Chapter 9

CHRIST'S LOVE IN MARRIAGE

Peter preached that in His suffering, Jesus left us an example, that we should follow His steps. "When He was insulted, He did not answer back with an insult; when He suffered, He did not threaten, but placed His hopes in God, the righteous Judge. Jesus carried our sins in His body to the cross, so that we might die to sin and live for righteousness. By His stripes we are healed" (1 Peter 2:23-24).

In the above scripture Peter gives Jesus' example of self-sacrificial love for the marriage relationship and encourages husbands and wives to love, honour and care for one another in the way Jesus does. Peter says, "Now that your souls have been cleansed from selfishness and hatred when you trusted Jesus to save you, see to it that you really do love each other warmly, with all your hearts" (1 Peter 1:22 TLB).

Why is marriage so fundamental in creation that Christ's Apostles likened the husband's love for his wife to that of Jesus Christ's love for the Church? The answer is that right from the beginning, through what happened to Adam and Eve, we can see that this divine union has been under attack and threatened to lose its God-given image of glory, with grave consequences for the next generation.

The Mystery of God in Marriage

When God called Abraham, He gave him an immense promise that in his Seed - Jesus - all the nations of the earth shall be blessed. Abraham believed God and his faith was accredited to him for righteousness, so that he became the father of many nations according to God's Word. However, like anyone living by faith, Abraham had to trust God to work His will by His Spirit in his relationship with his wife Sarah. It is so important for us to see how God worked in Abraham and Sarah's hearts over many years, so that they could give Him praise that what He had promised He was able to perform, although naturally this was impossible because they were both getting older and she was barren. Now look at how the power of God was at work in their marriage: God gave Abraham His Word, which enabled him to have faith for him and Sarah. Abraham learned through faith to have hope and not give up or look for another way, but to look to God who watches over His Word to perform it in him and Sarah. Sarah learned through faith to receive strength when all natural hope had died. She learned to trust God, who restores what is lost and who is always faithful to His Word. I pray you can see how they received the promised son according to God's Word!

The mystery of God in marriage is beautifully displayed in Abraham and Sarah, as through their union, God was able to bring forth His Promised Seed - Jesus - not by human might or power but by His Spirit; not by the will or ability of Abraham and Sarah, but by His Spirit working in their lives. Marriage is therefore given in creation that the husband and wife become one by God's Spirit to see Him work His perfect will in their lives and make them, and their children, and their children's children the heirs of His Life and blessings.

When Jesus was asked, "What is the greatest commandment given unto men?" He answered, "The first of all the commandments is: 'Hear, O Israel, the Lord our God, the Lord is one. And you shall love the Lord your God with all your heart, with all your soul, with all your mind, and with all your strength.' This is the first commandment. And the second, like it, is this: 'You shall love your neighbour as yourself.' There is no other commandment greater than these" (Mark 12:29-31).

What is interesting is that when this commandment was given, God said, "These words which I command you today shall be in your heart. You shall whet and sharpen them so as to make them penetrate, and teach and impress them diligently upon the [minds and] hearts of your children and shall talk of them when you sit in your house, when you walk by the way, when you lie down, and when you rise up" (Deuteronomy 6:6-7 AMPC). Can you see that our love for God is to be lived at home, so that our children can learn by what they see in us, how to love the Lord with all their heart, soul, mind and strength and how to love one another. I am so grateful for God's precious promises to those who trust Him to bless their children and their children's children! (Read Psalm 128 TLB.)

"As for Me this is My promise to them," says the Lord: "My Holy Spirit shall not leave them, and they shall want the good and hate the wrong - they and their children and their children's children forever" (Isaiah 59:21 TLB).

God's Gift of Oneness

When someone asked Jesus about marriage, He said, "Haven't you read the scripture that says that in the beginning the Creator made people male and female? And God said, 'For this reason a man will leave his father and mother and unite with his wife, and the two will become one.' So they are no longer two, but one. Man must not separate, then, what God has joined together" (Matthew 19:4-6 TEV). It is interesting that the exact word for God being One in Deuteronomy 6 is the same word Jesus uses for the husband and wife being made one in marriage. Oneness in marriage is God's gift (Malachi 2:15)!

Jesus shows us what this oneness looks like when He prayed, "Father, I have given them the glory You gave Me - the glorious unity of being one, as we are - I in them and You in Me, all being perfected into one - so that the world will know You sent Me and will understand that You love them as much as you love Me" (John 17:22-23 TLB).

Jesus is the perfect example of a husband's love for his wife and shows God's plan for man in His self-sacrificial love. When Jesus came into the world He said, "Even the Son of Man did not come to be served, but to serve, and to give His Life a ransom for many" (Mark 10:45). Jesus demonstrated the purity of His love - God's love - by His generosity as He gave up His glory and sweetly and quietly laid down His Life to serve. As it is written, "He endured the suffering that should have been ours, the pain that we should have borne. Because of our sins He was wounded, beaten because of the evil we did. We are healed by the punishment He suffered and made whole by the blows He received. Because the Lord made the punishment we deserved fall on Him" (Isaiah 53:4-6 TEV). "Now husbands are called to love their wives, just as Jesus loved the church and gave Himself for her" (Ephesians 5:25).

The husband is to be the priest of the home, rising early to pray, as he stands in the gap to see God's grace enable him, with a tender heart, to bear his wife's and children's burdens and so uphold and serve them with the Father's love. When a husband follows Jesus' example of self-sacrificial love and sweetly lays down his life to serve, he will see the Holy Spirit enable him to be of one spirit with his wife, sharing the grace of God as heirs together of Christ's Life, learning how to work together with one heart, mind and purpose to see all God's goodness and blessings in their marriage, their children and their children's children.

Peter said, "Husbands, likewise, dwell with them with understanding, giving honour to the wife, as to the weaker vessel, and as being heirs together of the grace of Life, that your prayers may not be hindered." And to the wife, Peter says, "Do not let your adornment be merely outward - arranging the hair, wearing gold, or putting on fine apparel - rather, let it be the hidden person of the heart, with the incorruptible beauty of a gentle and quiet spirit, which is very precious in the sight of God. For in this manner, in former times, the holy women who trusted in God also adorned themselves, being submissive to their own husbands" (1 Peter 3:7, 2-5).

As for Me and My House

While there is so much more to say on the subject of marriage and ministry, I want to give two thoughts for you to mediate on.

Firstly, when the husband and wife are one in their marriage covenant, the children will never wonder whom they belong to - Mum or Dad. A house united in Jesus Christ is built on the Rock and will stand no matter how great the storms in life.

Secondly, when a man lives the Life of Christ at home, his prayers will have great power and his preaching will give glory to God, especially in the heart of his wife and children, who know he lives at home - in private - what he preaches in public.

You may ask yourself, how is it ever possible for me to live this way? The answer is simply to see the Father form His Son in you by the Holy Spirit. Peter said, "As you know Jesus better, He will give you, through His great power, everything you need for living a truly good, godly Life: He will even share His own glory and His own goodness with you! And by that same mighty power, He gives you all the other rich and wonderful blessings He promised; for instance, the promise to save you from the lust and rottenness all around you, and to give you His own character" (2 Peter 1:3-4 TLB).

As I am writing this, my heart overflows with the Father's love, knowing that as you read, He is pouring His love into your heart by the Holy Spirit to enable you to love even as He loves. So that, as it is written, you can boldly say, "As for me and my house, we will serve the Lord" (Joshua 24:15).

Selah.
Take a moment and worshipfully meditate on this and the Holy Spirit will refresh you in your union with the Father and the Son, who is Jesus Christ our Lord.

Chapter 10

THE FATHER'S PROVISION

Right from the beginning, when Peter came to know Jesus, he learned from Him to trust God to meet his needs and to bless him over and above what he could achieve in his own strength. Peter learned to live by the spirit of faith that gives you the inward knowing that God will provide.

Remember when Jesus asked Peter for his boat so that he could use it as a place from which to preach to the crowds. After He had stopped speaking, He said to Peter, "Launch out into the deep and let down your nets for a catch." But Peter answered and said to Him, "Master, we have toiled all night and caught nothing, nevertheless at Your word I will let down the net." And when they had done this, they caught such a great number of fish that their nets were breaking. So, they signalled to their partners in the other boat to come and help them. And they came and filled both the boats, so that they began to sink. When Peter saw it, he fell at Jesus' knees, saying, "Depart from me, for I am a sinful man, O Lord!" For he and all who were with him were astonished at the catch of fish which they had taken; and so also were James and John, the sons of Zebedee, who were partners with Peter. And Jesus said to Peter, "Do not be afraid. From now on you will catch men." So, when they had brought their boats to land, they forsook all and followed Him (Luke 5:4-11).

All Christ's Apostles knew how to work hard and see God bless the work of their hands to provide for them and their loved ones. But they also knew how to leave it all behind to follow Jesus. Peter said to Jesus, "See, we have left all and followed You." Jesus answered and said to Peter, "Assuredly, I say to you, there is no one who has left house or brothers or sisters or father or mother or wife or children or lands, for My sake and the gospel's, who shall not receive a hundredfold now in this time - houses and brothers and sisters and mothers and children and lands, with persecutions - and in the age to come, Eternal Life" (Mark 10:28-30). What qualified Christ's Apostles to make Jesus known in the power of the Holy Spirit, was their unadulterated love for Him. Jesus said, "he who loves Me will be loved by My Father, and I will love him and manifest Myself to him" (John 14:21).

Just before He went to heaven, the scripture says, "Jesus showed Himself again to the disciples at the Sea of Tiberius and in this way He showed Himself: The disciples had worked all night but caught nothing. Then Jesus said to them, 'Cast the net on the right side of the boat, and you will find some.' So they cast their nets and now they were not able to draw it in because of the multitude of fish." Again and again, the Apostles learned that God gives power to prosper to those whose love is stayed on Him.

After this miraculous catch of fish, Jesus asked Peter three times if he loved Him more than all of these, that he should keep his eyes on the task of his Apostleship (John 21). Jesus said, "Your heavenly Father knows that you need all these things. But seek first the kingdom of God and His righteousness, and all these things shall be added to you" (Matthew 6:32-34).

What I Have, I Give

After Jesus had gone to heaven, Peter went to the temple to pray together with John. As they were about to enter the temple they saw a lame man at the gate begging. Fixing his eyes on him, with John, Peter said, "Look at us." So he gave them his attention, expecting to receive something from them. Then Peter said, "Silver and gold I do not have, but what I do have I give you: In the name of Jesus Christ of Nazareth, rise up and walk." And he took him by the right hand and lifted him up, and immediately his feet and ankle bones received strength. So he, leaping up, stood and walked and entered the temple with them - walking, leaping, and praising God (Acts 3:4-8).

Jesus said, "Every man is a fool who gets rich on earth but not in heaven" (Luke 12:21 TLB). You can see Peter's giving heart and how rich he had become in Jesus to be able to give such a lavish gift of healing to this man who had been lame from birth. The scripture says, "A generous man devises generous things, and by generosity he shall stand" (Isaiah 32:8). Peter knew this gift of healing did not come because of his own power or godliness but that it came straight from the rich treasury of Jesus Christ's glory in heaven. He also knew that the lame man had received his healing by faith in Jesus' name.

When some time later a man called Simon - a converted sorcerer - sought to obtain the gift of the Holy Spirit by offering Peter money, Peter said to him, "Your money perish with you, because you thought that the gift of God could be purchased with money! You have neither part nor portion in this matter, for your heart is not right in the sight of God. Repent therefore of this your wickedness... For I see that you are poisoned by bitterness and bound by iniquity" (Acts 8:18-23). Peter shows that earthly created things do not equal the value of the souls of men, nor can the gifts of God be bought. For not one of those who trust in their wealth and boast about how rich they are, though rich as kings, could ransom even his own brother from the penalty of sin! God's forgiveness does not come that way. A soul is far too precious to be ransomed by mere earthly wealth. There is not enough of it in all the earth to buy Eternal Life for just one soul and keep it from going to hell. The rich, the wise and powerful have no greater lease on life than anyone else. But the Psalmist says, "As for me, God will redeem my soul from the power of death, for He will receive me" (Psalm 49:15 TLB).

Rich in Jesus

I pray that you can see how rich Peter had become in Jesus - that His Life-giving Spirit flowed unhindered from him, as they even brought the sick out into the streets and laid them on beds and couches, that at least the shadow of Peter passing by might fall on some of them. Multitudes gathered from the surrounding cities to Jerusalem, bringing sick people and those who were tormented by unclean spirits, and they were all healed (Acts 5:14-16). I know that what you see in Peter is given to Christ's Apostles today, by the power of the Holy Spirit, to convince a new generation to believe in Jesus who is the same; yesterday, today and forever.

I would love to continue writing about Peter, as there is so much more to say about His Apostleship, and therefore I encourage you to daily read his inspired writings in the scriptures, as Peter's Apostolic ministry will unveil Jesus in you by the power of the Holy Spirit. There are many things Peter did and said that identifies him as an Apostle, but remember this - first and foremost Peter is Christ's Apostle because the Father was pleased to reveal His Son in him, so that when he spoke and masterfully opened the scriptures about Jesus, all who heard him and believed in Jesus received the Holy Spirit and were given a new birth as sons and daughters of God.

Selah.
Take a moment and worshipfully meditate on this and the Holy Spirit will refresh you in your union with the Father and the Son, who is Jesus Christ our Lord.

Part 3
JOHN, CHRIST'S APOSTLE

Chapter 11

THE FATHER'S LOVE

John's Apostleship radiates with the brilliant Light of the Life of Jesus Christ; the living expression of the Father, in Whom the Father is visible and made known. It is beautiful to see how the work that the Father gives to one Apostle, like John, differs from the work given to another Apostle, like Peter. However, it is unmistakably clear that they are both Christ's Apostles and that the Father is the One who enabled them.

Times of Maturing

In the beginning it seemed the work given to Peter was much greater than what was given to John. Peter's Apostolic ministry took off with great power when he, full of the Holy Spirit and fire, stood up on the Day of Pentecost and thousands of precious souls responded to His preaching. John, however, was pleased to stand alongside Peter and support what God was working through him. You can see the heart of Jesus being formed in John by how he was able to acknowledge, support and become one with what God was working through Peter.

I love Peter's passionate heart for Jesus, but he did not come into this ministry of Jesus without having to overcome some painful struggles. One time, when he saw John following Jesus, Peter asked the question, "Lord what about this man?" Jesus answered by saying, "If I will that he remains till I come, what is that to you? You follow Me" (John 21:21-22).

During times of maturing, while the stature and fullness of Christ's Life is being formed in you and His Life-giving

Word becomes active, powerful, and sharp, it can be a painful distraction to look at what God has given to another person and compare yourself, feel inferior, or even afraid and uncertain about what He has for you in His service. At these times it is important to always remember that God makes you what you ought to be, and that it is He who establishes you in Jesus as His Apostle. By His Spirit working in you, God helps you learn how to grow deep roots into Jesus Himself as you daily draw your nourishment for living, as He lives, from your union with Him. God wants you securely grounded and completely settled in Jesus, so that you know through experience the Life you now live is not your own but a gift of God, and that this Life is freely and continuously given by His grace through Jesus who is your Life.

Called, Chosen and Sent

When you consider what God has called you to, remember that He does all things according to the foreknowledge and pre-planned purpose of His good will. As it says in the Scriptures, those whom God has called He also foreknew (Romans 8:29). Look at these two examples. God said to Jeremiah, "Before I formed you in the womb, I knew you; before you were born, I sanctified you; I ordained you a prophet to the nations" (Jeremiah 1:5). Then King David said, "You saw me before I was born. Every day of my life was recorded in Your book. Every moment was laid out before a single day had passed." And while David said these things prophetically about Jesus, it was no less his own experience too (Psalm 139:16 NLT).

One identifiable quality in all Christ's Apostles is that they have an inward knowing that they are called of God, chosen, and sent by Him. Remember that Jesus prayed,

"Father I have manifested Your name to the men whom You have given Me out of the world. They were Yours. You gave them to Me" (John 17:6). Jesus knew the Father would show Him those who were given to Him, who were called and chosen to be His Apostles. "So, He went out to the mountain to pray, and continued all night in prayer to God. And when it was day, He called His disciples to Himself; and from them He chose twelve whom He also named Apostles (Luke 6:12-13). Jesus said to the twelve, "You did not choose Me, but I chose you and appointed you that you should go and bear fruit, and that your fruit should remain, that whatever you ask the Father in My Name, as representing Me, He may give you" (John 15:16).

The Scripture says, "Those whom God had already chosen He also set apart to become like His Son, so that the Son would be the first among many brothers. And so those whom God set apart, He called; and those He called, He put right with Himself and shared His glory with them. In view of all this, what can we say? If God is for us, who can be against us?" (Romans 8:29-31 TEV). This is one reason why Christ's Apostles were able to withstand such fierce opposition and overcome painful weaknesses in their own nature, because they had this deep-seated sense of God's calling that never faded or diminished from when they first became aware of it, but rather grew stronger and stronger - so much so that they did not even count their own lives dear to themselves, that they might fulfil the ministry which they received from the Lord Jesus, to testify to the gospel of the grace of God (Acts 20:24).

Formed and Fashioned by God

Christ's Apostles not only know God has called, chosen, and sent them; they also know that He is their maker. As it is written, "Know that the Lord, He is God; It is He who has made us, and not we ourselves; We are His people and the sheep of His pasture" (Psalm 100:3). Whilst God makes you, by conforming you inwardly into the image of His Son, He forms spiritual gifts in you - these special abilities have everything to do with what He has called you to do as a representative of Jesus.

Let me ask you a question, you who read the Scriptures - would you consider that John was given less in the kingdom of God than Peter or the other Apostles? Certainly not! The synoptic (i.e. similar) Gospels of Matthew, Mark and Luke are truly wonderful accounts, but John's Gospel stands out with such Apostolic grace that what is unveiled through it can only come from the loving, humble heart of Jesus that God was able to form in John. Remember that John was called "the disciple whom Jesus loved," not because Jesus loved him more than the others, but simply because John lived in His love.

When Jesus hung on the cross and "saw His mother, and the disciple whom He loved standing by, He said to His mother, "Woman, behold your son!" Then He said to the disciple, "Behold your mother!" And from that hour that disciple took her to his own home" (John 19:26-27). What Jesus gave John was most wonderful. He entrusted him with the care of His mother Mary. This was no small privilege but also no small responsibility considering that Mary had four other sons - James, Joseph, Simon, and Jude - who at first did not believe Jesus was the Son of God (Matthew 13:55; John 7:5). While they sought to be with Jesus, their unbelief and disjointed spirits gave rise to a power struggle that tried to undermine the works of God in Jesus. They scoffed when they said to Jesus, "Go where more people can see your miracles!" "You can't be famous when You hide like this! If You're so great, prove it to the world!" Jesus replied, "It is not the right time for Me to go now. But you can go anytime and it will make no difference, for the world can't hate you; but it does hate Me, because I accuse it of sin and evil. You go on, and I'll come later when it is the right time." So, He remained in Galilee" (John 7:3-9 TLB).

The responsibility of family life and ministry can be no small task to manage well, and without God's grace I would say it is impossible. Sure, it was a great privilege for Jesus to ask John to take care of His mother Mary, but at the same time on a more practical note it was not a short-term or easy responsibility.

Like John, we all go through times of preparation in our lives where we find ourselves in a place of responsibility during which the Father forms His character and His divine nature in us, whilst at the same time forming gifts of His Spirit in us, so we can learn to live and minister by the ability He supplies.

Communing with the Father

Without doubt, a training ground for all Christ's Apostles to see Christ formed in them is in their own home, in relation with those who are nearest, where because of familiarity, it is more difficult to hide from what's really living inside. The link between the way you live at home and the way you operate in public ministry cannot be over-emphasised, because as much as lives in you will come out of you.

One of the first lessons Jesus taught His Apostles was that what God sees in secret He rewards in public. Jesus said, "When you have shut your door, pray to your Father who is in the secret place; and your Father who sees in secret will reward you openly" (Matthew 6:6). All Christ's Apostles were men of prayer, and not just a little here and there in preparation for a meeting, but through a daily prayer-life they learned how to draw their nourishment for Life and ministry from their union with the Father and the Son.

You can see how Jesus led the way into this Life of prayer and communion with the Father right from the start, when He came up from the water after being baptised by John the Baptist. When Jesus prayed, heaven opened, the Holy Spirit descended in the appearance of a dove, alighting on Jesus. Then the Father was heard saying to Him; "You are My Beloved Son; in You I am well pleased!" (Luke 3:21-22). This beautiful Life of communion with the Father endured through all His days on earth. Indeed, Jesus often prayed all night and early in the morning. He prayed on the Mount of Transfiguration and in the Garden of Gethsemane, with many tears and loud cries, the night before he died on the cross. Now that Jesus is in heaven and ever lives to make intercession, the Father longs to draw you up into the Life that Jesus has with Him, so that you may develop a daily prayer life in the unspeakable joy of His Son's Life of perfect communion with Him and see this Life revealed in you here on earth. No Apostle will see the more excellent ministry of the Life-giving Spirit of Jesus without communion with the Father and the Son in a daily prayer life; and no Apostle is an Apostle without this Life being manifest in and through him by the power of the Holy Spirit.

It takes time to learn that you cannot lean on your authority as an Apostle, nor on the power you experience when you share the Word and minister in the gifts of the Holy Spirit. Like Jesus, who lived in unbroken communion with the Father, your Life and ministry must come forth out of the secret place of the Most High, your prayer closet, where you live in fellowship with the Father and the Son and are continually endued and renewed with the richest measure of the Divine presence, the Life-giving Spirit of Jesus, the Anointing - the unction of the Holy One.

Jesus knew that what He asked John to do in taking care of His mother Mary involved a responsibility for His natural brothers and sisters as well, however Jesus knew this was entrusted to John by the Father. For me, this is one of the most beautiful graces of the loving heart of the Father, that what He asks you to do He also makes you willing and able to do. While this takes time, as you learn how to develop a daily prayer life, God is the One who will work in you by His Spirit to make your sense of inability and powerlessness to bear the burdens of responsibility a plea in prayer. Thus you will see the wonder of Him making you able by forming His gifts in you. And what I find most glorious in all of this is that you become more and more like Jesus through it all.

Remember when Jesus said, "Most assuredly, I say to you, the Son can do nothing of Himself, but what He sees the Father do; for whatever He does, the Son also does in like manner. For the Father loves the Son and shows Him all things that He Himself does; and He will show Him greater works than these, that you may marvel. For as the Father raises the dead and gives Life to them, even so the Son gives Life to whom He will" (John 5:19-21). This shows you that Jesus is like the Father through the works He does.

Jesus said, "The works which the Father has given Me to finish - the very works that I do - bear witness of Me, that the Father has sent Me" (John 5:36). "Do you not believe that I am in the Father, and the Father in Me? The words that I speak to you I do not speak on My own authority; but the Father who dwells in Me does the works. Believe Me that I am in the Father and the Father in Me, or else believe Me for the sake of the works themselves" (John 14:10-11). Then Jesus said something most wonderful: "Most assuredly, I say to you, he who believes in Me, the works that I do he will do also; and greater works than these he will do, because I go to My Father. And whatever you ask in My name, that I will do, that the Father may be glorified in the Son. If you ask anything in My name, I will do it" (John 14:12-14). Let me say this again so that you can clearly see what Jesus is saying to you: whatever you ask the Father "representing Me", that He will do, so that the Father may be glorified through His Son in you. Can you see that just as Jesus is identified as One sent - representing the Father - so Christ's Apostles are identified as being sent - representing Jesus - by the works they do?

When John was still young and did not yet know the works the Father had prepared for him, he came to Jesus with his mother Salome and brother James, who also would become an Apostle. His mother asked Jesus if her sons could sit at His right and left hand in the kingdom, and Jesus said to her, "You don't know what you are asking for." Then He looked to John and James and asked them, "Can you drink the cup of suffering that I am about to drink?" "We can," they answered. "You will indeed drink from My cup," Jesus told them, "but I do not have the right to choose who will sit at My right and My left. These places belong to those for whom My Father has prepared them" (Matthew 20:22-23 TEV). May this deeply penetrate your heart: Jesus said that these places belong to those "for whom My Father has prepared them"! It is exciting to know that God has prepared a place for you in His kingdom, but it is just as exciting to know that He is preparing you for that place right now.

An Apostle of Love

When you read the Holy Scriptures written by John, he clearly stands out from the other Apostles in his ability to unveil the loving heart of God the Father in Jesus the Son. John writes with a heavenly language that only those who are taught by the Spirit of the Father can fully appreciate.

The Holy Spirit was able to form this ability in him during many years of preparation. We know this because John did not write the Gospel of John and his other New Testament writings until much later in life, most likely not until about 85 AD. However, God began to prepare John's heart even from before his birth, fashioning it for His purposes.

What undoubtedly played an important role in his life is that his mother Salome loved Jesus and is even thought to be the younger sister of Mary the mother of Jesus. In fact, it is likely that the wedding in Cana, where Jesus did His first miracle to show His glory with the Father when He turned water into wine, was John's wedding. While there may be some debate about whether his mother was the younger sister of Mary, and whether the wedding in Cana was his own wedding, what is certain is that there are many things through which the divine influence prepared the heart of John. We can see how John the Baptist's burning, shining light had a great impact on him, as his divinely inspired words lived in John's heart. If you read John 3:27-36, you will see how John remembered these words. I thank God for those who, like John the Baptist, are sent to prepare the hearts of His servants.

A Heart Prepared by and for God

I believe that in every generation God's voice is calling for new labourers through those who have His grace, His divine ability to help others rise to their God-given place; those who, like John the Baptist, can point them in the right direction by helping them to see that Jesus is the Lamb of God who came to take away the sin of the world and that He is the One who will baptise you with the Holy Spirit and fire. Personally, I find doing this kind of work a great privilege. However, it is not something we can do in our own strength, "for a man can receive nothing unless it has been given to him from heaven" (John 3:27). It is obvious to see from John's life that what John the Baptist imparted to him came from the Father in heaven. I believe there is a great need today - as there always has been and always will be - for those like John the Baptist, through whom God can work to prepare those whom He is calling into His service!

In John you can see how God prepares you by what His Spirit inclines your heart to and by what He enables you to hear and see. John was able to see that Jesus is the living expression of the Father; the One who came forth from the Father to reveal the Father, and to make Him known in Himself; for all that Jesus is, says and does reveals that He is God, that He is the Light of Life who gives Life to all living things, for He created all things and by the Light of His Life they exist. However, when the author of all that has been created came into the world, He was not recognised nor received by His own. But as many as receive Him are given His Life-giving power to become sons and daughters of God, who are born not merely of a natural birth but who are born of God.

I pray that you can see in John the priceless privilege of being Christ's Apostle. I also pray that in John you can see the overwhelming preciousness, the surpassing worth, and supreme advantage of knowing Jesus and of progressively becoming more deeply and intimately acquainted with Him; having such a heart prepared by and for God so that you can perceive and recognise the wonder of His person in yourself and others. If God can give John such a beautiful heart, then be encouraged to wait on Him and not be weary in whatever place of responsibility you may find yourself. For it is where you are right now that the Father is forming His Son in you, to prepare you to make Him known in all you are, say and do by the power of the Holy Spirit.

Waiting for God's Timing

If you need some reassurance concerning the work that God has prepared for you in His service, then look to Jesus! Remember when Mary asked Jesus for help because they had run out of wine at the wedding in Cana, Galilee? Jesus said to His mother, "How does that concern Me? My time has not yet come" (John 2). What Jesus was saying here is most important for you to receive within yourself. He said, "If I do this now it will change everything for Me, for I am only to come out from being hidden to reveal My glory with the Father at His appointed time."

Jesus knew how to wait on God, for as the Son of Man, He knew He could do nothing apart from the Father. Jesus had no doubt the Father loved Him, so there was no fear in Him but rather the complete rest that comes from believing that the Father would show Him what to do. Even when His mother Mary pulled on His divine ability to act, Jesus waited and searched within Himself to see what the Father would show Him. When this spirit of faith, of waiting on God, that you see in Jesus is lacking in His servants, and the ability which God supplies has not sufficiently been formed and matured in them, they can be tempted to act presumptuously and become vulnerable to please man, rather than God.

I remember when I started to minister the Word of God in 1978. I had just turned eighteen years of age. Earlier that year Jesus appeared to me in a vision when I had broken my neck in two places in a car accident. He asked me, "Robert, what have you done for Me in your life?" Even though I could not answer Him because I had been living in sin, Jesus mercifully healed me when my father, Johan Maasbach, prayed for me. When I walked out of the hospital only three days later, my father, who himself was a great Apostle of the Lord Jesus, said to me, "Now you know your life is not your own!" Then he said, "Robert, don't be too concerned about what you will do for God. Just be sure He knows where to find you."

Remember, God found King David while he was a shepherd taking care of his father's sheep, trusting Him to give him victory when a lion or bear attacked the flock. The scripture says, "I have found David the son of Jesse, a man after My own heart, who will do all My will. With My holy oil I have anointed him" (Acts 13:22; Psalm 89:20). God chose His servant David and took him from looking after his father's flocks and made him king of Israel and the shepherd of His people. The Bible says that David took care of them with unselfish devotion and led them with skill (Psalm 78).

All Christ's Apostles have their own journey of preparation. At the time of writing this, it has only been forty years after I had the vision of Jesus calling me into His service - and I feel as if I am just beginning. I pray that your tender heart will know that "the God of peace, who brought again from the dead our Lord Jesus, will equip you with all you need for doing His perfect will. May Jesus who became the great Shepherd of the sheep by an everlasting agreement between God and you, signed with His blood, produce in you through His power all that is pleasing to Him. To Him be glory forever and ever. Amen" (Hebrews 13:20-21 TLB).

Just keep your eyes on Jesus, for everything that happened in and through Him fulfilled God's good Word. This shows you that as you trust the Father, like Jesus, and rest in His Providence, He is able to carry out His purposes in and through your life. Never forget, no matter where you are or what responsibility you bear, that there is no real glory in life and ministry except that the Father reveals His Son in you, so that the life you live and the grace you give is not your own but a gift of God. Remember that all Christ's Apostles learned from Jesus to rest in the Father's love and to be satisfied, fulfilled and found faithful in whatever place of responsibility He had given them.

Selah.
Take a moment and worshipfully meditate on this and the Holy Spirit will refresh you in your union with the Father and the Son, who is Jesus Christ our Lord.

Chapter 12

A TENDER HEART

One of the main characteristics I would like you to see in John is how important it is to have a tender heart. When you live filled with the Holy Spirit, His blessed presence and comfort is what makes you tender-hearted, so you are able by the Spirit to know, perceive, acknowledge, and recognise Jesus and hear His voice.

Jesus was often burdened when His disciples' hearts were still hard, and they did not know Him. Remember how with five loaves and two fish, Jesus fed five thousand hungry men - not including all the women and children - and how His disciples gathered twelve baskets of leftovers. After this, Jesus went up onto the mountain to pray while He sent His disciples across the lake. At the fourth night watch, which is about three in the morning, the disciples were struggling against the wind and had only been able to row for three to four miles. It was then that Jesus came to them walking on the water. This frightened them so much that they cried out, thinking they were seeing a ghost. But Jesus said, "Be of good cheer! It is I; do not be afraid." Then Peter answered Him and said, "Lord, if it is You, command me to come to You on the water." So, He said, "Come." And when Peter had come down out of the boat, he walked on the water to Jesus. But when he saw that the wind was boisterous, he was afraid; and beginning to sink he cried out, saying, "Lord, save me!" Immediately, Jesus stretched out His hand and caught him, and said to him, "O you of little faith, why did you doubt?" And when they got into the boat, the wind ceased (Matthew 14:27-32). The Gospel of Mark says, that when Jesus came into the boat with Peter the disciples were "greatly amazed in themselves beyond measure, and marvelled. For they had not understood about the loaves, because their hearts were hardened" (Mark 6:51-52).

What does it mean, "Their hearts were hardened"? The Bible describes a hard heart as the heart of someone who has eyes to see but cannot perceive, and ears to hear but cannot understand. The disciples' hearts were hard in that they saw the Spirit of Life in Jesus when He multiplied the loaves, but when He came to them walking on the water they did not recognise Him; they did not know Him inwardly in their spirit.

I love Peter's passion to know Jesus and to follow Him, when he cries out, "Lord if it is You, command me to come to You." Peter suffered some painful failures in the development of the gift given him by the Father to know Jesus. One of the well-known failures Peter suffered was after being warned by Jesus and encouraged to pray lest he enter into temptation, he three times denied that he knew Him. I say this to encourage you, so that like Peter you will never give up - never let your weaknesses or failures stop you - for the Father will perfect that which concerns you in His service. Jesus loves you and He will reveal Himself *to* you and *in* you (Matthew 16:16-17; John 14:21).

Feeding on the Life Jesus gives

In his gospel, John unveils what Jesus was saying through the miraculous provision of bread, because the next day, when the people who ate the bread found Jesus, He said to them, "Most assuredly, I say to you, you seek Me because you ate of the loaves and were filled. Do not labour for the food which perishes, but for the food which endures to everlasting Life, which the Son of Man will give you, because God the Father has set His seal on Him" (John 6:27; Isaiah 55:1-3).

What Jesus is saying is so important to understand. The bread they ate, yes it was given by a miracle, but it did not produce Spirit Life in them for they had no faith to recognise and know God even though He was clearly visible to them in Jesus. The miracle they experienced had not changed their hearts. For that to happen they needed to have a new birth and receive a spiritually alive heart by feeding on the Life Jesus gives. This is why Jesus said to them, "I am the bread of Life. He who comes to Me shall never hunger, and he who believes in Me shall never thirst. For as the living Father sent Me, and I live because of the Father, so he who feeds on Me will live because of Me" (John 6:35-36, 57).

What I am showing you can easily be misunderstood when so many focus their message on the supernatural provision of our natural needs and desires, which you can see in Jesus multiplying the five loaves and two fish to feed the multitude, that God is more than willing and able to meet. However, the first and foremost grace given to Christ's Apostles is to demonstrate in the power of the Holy Spirit that Jesus is the true Life-giving bread who has come down from the Father, and that as you feed on Him and let your roots grow deep into Him, by daily drawing your nourishment for Life and ministry from your union with Him, you will learn to live as He lives, in perfect fellowship with the Father, and have the ability to know, perceive, acknowledge and recognise Him inwardly and in others.

Judging Others by the Spirit

It is beautiful to see the loving humble heart of Jesus being formed in John as he faithfully took care of His mother Mary and the family and worked alongside Peter. John's humble heart was given such grace by the Lord Jesus that he was not easily moved by power struggles in the family or ministry but rather he was a calming and a unifying force.

This is no small work of God's grace in John when you consider that Jesus called him and his brother James, "sons of thunder" (Mark 3:17). When Jesus sent them to prepare the way for His coming, and they encountered some opposition they said, "Lord, do You want us to command fire to come down from heaven and consume them, just as Elijah did?" Jesus had to rebuke them saying, "You do not know what manner of spirit you are of. For the Son of Man did not come to destroy men's lives but to save them" (Luke 9:54-56). What John received through his union with Jesus is a most important Apostolic gift. John could see that Jesus did not judge anyone by what He saw or heard, but the Father's love enabled Him to receive those the Father gave and entrusted to Him, so that through being with Jesus they might come to find, know, and see the only true living God in Him.

Isaiah tells us how the Holy Spirit enabled Jesus to only do what the Father showed Him when He says, "And the Spirit of the Lord shall rest upon Him, the Spirit of wisdom, understanding, counsel, and might; the Spirit of knowledge and of the fear of the Lord. And shall make Him of quick understanding, and His delight shall be in the reverential and obedient fear of the Lord. And He shall not judge by the sight of His eyes, neither decide by the hearing of His ears. He will not judge by appearance, false evidence, or hearsay, but will defend the poor and the exploited. He will rule against the wicked who oppress them. For He will be clothed with fairness and with truth" (Isaiah 11:2-5 TLB/AMP).

Jesus shows you how to trust the Father in His great love for others and how not to judge them by what you see or hear, but to know them as He knows them. Jesus said, "I am the good Shepherd. As the Father knows Me and I know the

Father, in the same way I know My sheep and they know Me. And I am willing to die for them" (John 10:14-15 TEV). This kind of knowing people by the Spirit, to have the mind you see in Jesus, is one of the great graces by which not just Christ's Apostles but all God's servants are given to love the people whom they serve.

You can clearly see that through His abiding in the Father's love Jesus did not need anyone to tell Him what was in a man for He knew what was in everyone's heart (1 Samuel 16:7; John 2:24-25). One great hindrance to being able to see what God sees in others is being moved by what they are like after their natural nature or by hearsay, presumption, assumption, or suspicion. Such character flaws have nothing in common with what you see in Jesus. For Christ's Apostles to have this ability you see in Jesus, of how to judge others by the Spirit, takes more time to develop than some of the other graces of His divine nature, for it demands very deep roots of His Spirit in them.

Jesus said, "I am able to do nothing from Myself [independently, of My own accord - but only as I am taught by God and as I get His orders]. Even as I hear, I judge [I decide as I am bidden to decide. As the voice comes to Me, so I give a decision], and My judgment is right (just, righteous), because I do not seek or consult My own will [I have no desire to do what is pleasing to Myself, My own aim, My own purpose] but only the will and pleasure of the Father Who sent Me" (John 5:30 AMPC).

The following Scripture moves me deeply considering how much the Father is willing to entrust to His servants. "I said, 'You are gods [since you judge on My behalf, as My representatives]; indeed, all of you are children of the Most High" (Psalm 82:6 AMPC). You can see from what Jesus is saying that when you abide in the Father's love, He frees you from thoughts and desires to live to please yourself and seek your own will, for the Father in His great love forms in you His perfect will as He enables you to hear His voice and be taught by Him.

For Christ's Apostles there is no greater pleasure and sense of fulfilment than what we see in Jesus, whose pleasure was to do the will of the Father. What is most important for you to see, is that the ability to judge righteously by the Spirit, which all Christ's Apostles must be able to do, lies at the root of Jesus abiding in the love of the Father and thereby being empowered and enabled by Him to know and do His perfect will.

Abiding in the Father's Love

You may say, but do you really believe that all Christ's Apostles can have this same abiding Life in the Father's love, to hear His voice and be taught by Him? Without a doubt they can! It is essential for Christ's Apostles that they abide with Jesus in the Father's love so that they may have the power to know and do His perfect will. Jesus said, "I have loved you, [just] as the Father has loved Me; abide in My love [continue in His love with Me]" (John 15:9 AMPC). Now Jesus says to you, "Come and abide in the Father's love with Me!" You may say, "But, how can I? I don't know the way." Jesus says to you, "I am the Way! As you abide in My love for you, I will fill you with the Father's love, until you become a body wholly filled and flooded with God Himself and will enjoy the richest measure of His presence" (Ephesians 3:19 AMPC).

Through His abiding in the Father's love, you can see that it was not in Jesus to seek His own glory or honour. Jesus said, "I am not in search of honour for Myself. [I do not seek and am not aiming for My own glory.] There is One Who [looks after that; He] seeks [My glory], and He is the

Judge. If I were to glorify Myself (magnify, praise, and honour Myself), I would have no real glory, for My glory would be nothing and worthless. [My honour must come to Me from My Father.] It is My Father Who glorifies Me [Who extols Me, magnifies, and praises Me], of Whom you say that He is your God" (John 8:50, 54 AMPC).

What you see here in Jesus is essential to seek within yourself through your abiding in His love. For as long as it is within you to seek your own honour, to crave for the praise and recognition of men rather than God, you will be hindered to know others by the Spirit and to love them from a pure heart and undefiled faith. Look at the Father's loving heart in Jesus and how the Father honoured Him when Jesus says, "All whom My Father gives (entrusts) to Me will come to Me; and the one who comes to Me I will most certainly not cast out [I will never, no never, reject one of them who comes to Me]. I have come down from heaven not to do My own will and purpose but to do the will and purpose of Him Who sent Me. And this is the will of Him Who sent Me, that I should not lose any of all that He has given Me, but that I should give new Life and raise [them all] up at the last day" (John 6:37-39 AMPC).

I must repeat this again, so you can clearly see the loving heart of the Father in Jesus and how the Father honoured Him. Jesus says, "No one can come to Me unless the Father who sent Me draws him. It is written in the prophets, 'And they shall all be taught by God.' Therefore, everyone who has heard and learned from the Father comes to Me" (John 6:44-45).

The Father's Love in us

Jesus prays, "Father, I have told these men about You. They were in the world, but then You gave them to Me. Actually they were always Yours, and You gave them to Me; and they have kept Your word. Now they know that everything I have is a gift from You, for I have passed on to them the words You gave Me; and they accepted them and know that I came from You, and they believe You sent Me. My prayer is for those You have given Me, because they belong to You. And all of them, since they are Mine, belong to You for You have given them to Me, so they are My glory" (John 17:6-10 NLT).

Without doubt, Jesus' prayer is what He is seeing the Father working in His Apostles. Jesus says, "Father all that is Mine is Yours, and all that is Yours belongs to Me. The glory You have given Me is revealed in them - they are My glory!" I pray that your heart overflows with the Father's love for those He has entrusted to you and that you may see Him working in them by His Spirit, drawing them to Jesus, so that you may rejoice as you are given to partake in the glory and honour the Father has given Jesus. I pray this deeply penetrates your heart, that it pleases the Lord Jesus to see you share the honour and glory He receives from the Father, in that the Father is working with you, drawing everyone to Jesus, so that through Him they may receive a warm welcome in His presence.

In His prayer Jesus shows three reasons why He loves us with the same love the Father loves Him. First, so that the world may realise the Father sent Him. Second, that we might realise the Father loves us as much as He loves Him. And third, that we might know Jesus living in us. Jesus finished His prayer by saying, "O righteous Father, the world doesn't know You, but I do; and these disciples know You sent Me because I have revealed You to them and will keep on revealing You, so that the same mighty love You have for Me may be in them, and I in them" (John 17:17).

The More Excellent Ministry

I know that what you are learning by what you see in Jesus may be difficult to comprehend or know how to put into practice. Without doubt the Holy Spirit is here to help you! We are so used to judging others, how shall I say, from a mere human perspective; but Jesus shows you His more excellent ministry. He loved and trusted others because He knew the Father had given them to Him, and that by becoming one with Him in the Spirit they would receive His Life and everything He has with the Father, and be transformed into His likeness. And what's more, Jesus' joy overflowed to see them share the love and glory He receives from the Father.

I find all this so wonderful and can truly say I would not be here to write these things if it were not for the unfailing love and faithfulness of Jesus, who called me and entrusted me with the work of His Life-giving ministry. Trust Jesus to teach, empower and enable you to love others as He loves you, for then your joy will be full! Jesus will never fail to share the glory and honour He receives from the Father with you and enable you to have faith and love for and in others, knowing nothing against them, even when the way they are is still so very human and earthly.

Jesus said the reason people misjudge others is because they don't know the love of the Father. Jesus was no stranger to being misjudged. He understood why people had such harsh, fault-finding thoughts. He says, "Your approval or disapproval means nothing to Me, because I know you don't have God's love within you. If God were your Father, you would love Me" (John 5:41-45, 8:42). Jesus said, "Those of you who seek God's glory are able to see that the words I speak are not from Myself but from the Father. I'm not teaching you My own thoughts, but those of God who sent

Me. If any of you really determines to do God's will, then you will certainly know whether My teaching is from God or is merely My own. Anyone presenting his own ideas is looking for praise for himself, but anyone seeking to honour the One who sent Him, His message is true for He is a good and true person" (John 14:10 NKJV, 7:16-18 TLB). "Do not judge according to appearance, but judge with righteous judgment" (John 7:24).

What Jesus is saying is this: as long as you judge Me with your human limitations, you won't know who I am; and if you don't know Me then this shows you don't know My Father. However, if you had known Me, you would have known My Father also; and from now on you know Him and have seen Him. He who has seen Me has seen the Father; believe that I am in the Father, and the Father is in Me.

Can you see that when your judgments are not formed by God's Spirit, you are blind to the Truth even when it is right before your eyes? And that when you seek recognition and praise from others rather than God the Father, you will struggle to see what He desires to show you. Jesus said, "How can you say you know God, whom you cannot see, when He is in Me whom you can see but Me you will not receive? How is it possible for you to believe [how can you learn to believe], you who [are content to seek and] receive praise and honour and glory from one another, and yet do not seek the praise and honour and glory which come from Him Who alone is God?" (John 5:44 AMPC). Jesus said, "I could condemn you for much and teach you much, but I won't, for I say only what I am told by the One who sent Me; and He is Truth" (John 8:26 TLB).

It is so important for you to see that however much the evil heart of unbelief caused the people to misjudge Jesus, the love of the Father enabled Him to hold back judgment and not condemn them. To have the ability to hold back judgment and not condemn comes from the love of the Father that you see in Jesus. Jesus held back judgment because He looked to the joy set before Him to become the author and finisher of our faith.

Oh, how great is the love with which Jesus loved us and gave Himself for us while we were yet sinners, so that He might fill our hearts with His love and faith to dispel the darkness of unbelief so that we might see God in Him.

Jesus loved His own and fervently desired to show them the extent of His love; that is why He said to them, "But that the world may know that I love the Father, and the Father loves them, as He gave Me commandment, so I do. When you lift up the Son of Man, then you will know that I am He, and that I do nothing of Myself; but as My Father taught Me, I speak these things. And He who sent Me is with Me. The Father has not left Me alone, for I always do those things that please Him." As He spoke these words, many believed in Him (John 13:1, 14:31, 3:16, 8:28-30).

Selah.
Take a moment and worshipfully meditate on this and the Holy Spirit will refresh you in your union with the Father and the Son, who is Jesus Christ our Lord.

Chapter 13

OPENING BLIND EYES

One of the most powerful sermons Jesus preached was to a Pharisee, a senator, a privy-councillor, a man who was called a "master," or "doctor" of the Law, a ruler of the Jews, a man of great authority in Jerusalem. His name was Nicodemus. He was a very wealthy member of the Sanhedrin. In fact, he was reputed to be so rich that he could support all the inhabitants of Jerusalem for ten years and have plenty left over.

Nicodemus came to Jesus by night and said to Him, "Rabbi, we know that You are a teacher come from God; for no one can do these signs that You do unless God is with him." Jesus answered and said to him, "Most assuredly, I say to you, unless one is born again, he cannot see the kingdom of God." When Nicodemus did not understand what Jesus meant by being "born again", Jesus said, unless a person is born of water and the Spirit, he cannot enter the kingdom of God (John 3:1-3).

Throughout Scripture, water is a powerful symbol for new Life; as when John reports that water as well as blood flowed from Jesus' pierced side - the water being His Spirit, and the blood His person (Jesus, the Son of Man). In water baptism, we all partake in His death as we are buried with Him and arise from the water made alive with Him. Last but not least, water flowed from the Rock in the Old Testament. Jesus is the Rock from Whom the water of His Life-giving Spirit flows, through Whom we are born again, born of God.

Jesus shows Nicodemus that natural birth comes through men, but only God, who is Spirit, can give a Spiritual birth. He shows him that when he is born again, he will be able to see in himself by the Spirit of God what he is seeing in Jesus and enter the kingdom of heaven. Nicodemus still did not understand and asked, "But how can these things be?" To open Nicodemus' eyes, Jesus used a familiar example from the Scriptures and said, "Remember when Moses lifted up the serpent in the wilderness, even so must the Son of Man be lifted up, that whoever believes in Him should not perish but have Eternal Life" (John 3:14-15). You see, because of the darkened hearts and moral decay arising from their unbelief, the people were bitten by serpents in the wilderness. Only when they acknowledged their sin by looking at the brass serpent (which God told Moses to erect on a wooden pole) were they healed. Only then were they saved from judgment. This is an example of what God would accomplish through Jesus, whom He made to be sin for us on the cross, so that anyone who in repentance looks to Him would be saved.

Jesus then began to share the reason He came, saying, "God so loved the world that He gave His only begotten Son, that whoever believes in Him should not perish but have everlasting Life. For God did not send His Son into the world to condemn, (judge, to pass sentence on) the world, but that the world through Him might be saved. He who believes in Him is not condemned; but he who does not believe is condemned already, because he has not believed in the name of the only begotten Son of God. And this is the condemnation, that the Light has come into the world, and men loved darkness rather than Light, because their deeds were evil. For everyone practicing evil hates the Light and does not come to the Light, lest his deeds should be exposed. But he who does the truth comes to the Light, that his deeds may be clearly seen, that they have been done in God" (John 3:16-21).

I trust you can see how Jesus opened Nicodemus' eyes. He opened his eyes by giving him the faith that if he believed in Him, he would be saved and receive Eternal Life - the Life he saw in Jesus. Nicodemus became a follower of Jesus and loved Him. Together with Joseph of Arimathea, he brought about one hundred pounds of spices - a mixture of myrrh and aloes - and the two men took Jesus' body down from the cross and wrapped it in linen cloths with the spices, according to the Jewish custom of preparing a body for burial. All this occurred so that the Scripture might be fulfilled saying, "And they made His grave with the wicked - but with the rich at His death, because He had done no violence, nor was any deceit in His mouth" (Isaiah 53:9). "Now there was a garden in the place where Jesus had been put to death, and in it there was a new tomb where no one had ever been buried. Since it was the day before the Sabbath and because the tomb was close by, they placed Jesus' body there" (John 19:39-42 TEV).

The Fountain of Living Water

John shows us that one of the great Apostolic gifts you see in Jesus is to open peoples' eyes to all God gives through Him. In chapter 7 of John, he shares about the great tradition on the last day of the Feast of Tabernacles for the priest to take a golden pitcher and draw some water from the Pool of Siloam, which he then poured on the altar in the temple while the people worshipped, singing, "O Lord, I will praise You; though You were angry with me, Your anger is turned away, and You comfort me. Behold, God is my salvation, I will trust and not be afraid; For YAH, the Lord, is my strength and song; He also has become my salvation. Therefore, with joy I will draw water from the wells of salvation" (Isaiah 12:1-3).

Oh, how precious are all these promises that find their fulfilment in our lives through Jesus, for while the people worshipped, Jesus cried out with a loud voice saying, "If anyone thirsts, let him come to Me and drink. He who believes in Me, as the Scripture has said, out of his heart will flow rivers of Living water." But this He spoke concerning the Spirit, whom those believing in Him would receive; for the Holy Spirit was not yet given, because Jesus was not yet glorified (John 7:37-39).

After this, Jesus spent the night on the Mount of Olives and came again into the Temple early in the morning. There Jesus was teaching the people when a woman caught in the act of adultery was brought before Him. They said to Him, "Teacher, this woman was caught in adultery, in the very act. Now Moses, in the law, commanded us that such should be stoned. But what do You say?" This they said, testing Him, that they might have something of which to accuse Him. But Jesus stooped down and wrote on the ground with His finger, as though He did not hear (John 8:3-6).

Jeremiah shows what Jesus was doing when He was writing in the dust, for he says, "O Lord, the hope of Israel, all who forsake You shall be ashamed. Those who depart from Me shall be written in the earth, because they have forsaken the Lord, the fountain of Living waters" (Jeremiah 17:13). So, when they continued asking Him, He raised Himself up, looked at all of them and said, "He who is without sin (sinful desires) among you, let him throw a stone at her first." And again, He stooped down and wrote on the ground. Then those being convicted by their conscience, went out one-by-one, beginning with the oldest even to the last. And Jesus was left alone, and the woman standing in the midst. When Jesus had raised Himself up and saw none but the woman, He said to her, "Woman, where are those accusers of yours? Has no one condemned you?" She said, "No one, Lord." Jesus said to her, "Neither do I condemn you; go and sin no more" (John 8:7-11).

Jesus, the fountain of Living waters, demonstrated the mercies and lovingkindness of God by setting this woman free from judgment, letting her walk away forgiven. To those who witnessed this display of mercy, He says, "If you abide in My Word, you are My disciples indeed. And you shall know the truth, and the truth shall make you free." They answered Him, "We are Abraham's descendants, and have never been in bondage to anyone. How can You say, 'You will be made free'?" Jesus answered them, "Most assuredly, I say to you, whoever commits sin is a slave of sin. And a slave does not abide in the house forever, but a son abides forever, therefore if the Son makes you free, you shall be free indeed" (John 8:31-36).

Can you see Jesus offered them to drink of the fountain of Living waters - the same water He gave to the woman whom He set free? None of them could cast the first stone, so they all needed the Living waters as much as she did, but when Jesus offered it to them they picked up stones to throw at Him, but He hid himself and left the Temple. It is painful to see those who are ready to condemn others, while blind to their own sins and need of forgiveness.

Wash and See!

Outside the Temple were the lame and blind, and while He was walking along, He saw a man who had been blind from birth. "Teacher," His disciples asked Him. "Why was this man born blind? Was it a result of his own sins or those of his parents?" "It was not because of his sins or his parents' sins," Jesus answered. "He was born blind so the power of God could be seen in him. All of us must quickly carry out the tasks assigned us by the One who sent Me, because there is little time left before the night falls and all work comes to an end. But while I am still here in the world, I am the

Light of the world." Then He spat on the ground, made mud with the saliva, and smoothed the mud over the blind man's eyes. He told him, "Go and wash in the pool of Siloam". So, the man went and washed, and came back seeing! (John 9:1-5 NLT).

What is interesting is that the word Siloam means "sent". The word "sent" is a link to the word "Apostle", whose root meaning is "one sent". So you see, Jesus desires His Apostles to open peoples' eyes to the salvation and new Life that they receive through faith in Him. At the same time, you can see how the mindset of Christ's Apostles still needed to be renewed, for they prejudged this man and his parents. What they saw and learned by being with Jesus was that instead of judging this man, He opened his eyes to demonstrate the Father's love.

Jesus said, "I have come to open the eyes of those who are blind and to help those who think they can see realise how spiritually blind they really are." Some of the Pharisees who heard these words said to Him, "Are You saying that we are blind?" Jesus said to them, "If you were blind, you would not realise what you are doing is sin; but now that you say, you can see, that means you know what you are doing and therefore you are guilty of sin" (John 9:39-41 NKJ/TLB).

Now consider what Jesus was saying by sending the blind man to the Pool of Siloam to wash. Remember the priest just a day before, on the last day of the great feast, had taken this water and poured it on the altar while the people were singing that God was no longer angry but that He had become their salvation and strength so that they could come and draw from the well of salvation with joy. Remember that at the same time, Jesus cried out that if anyone was thirsty, they should come to Him and drink from the Life-giving water, the Holy Spirit He gives. So, what Jesus is saying by sending the blind man to this water to wash, is that those who believe in Him will see in themselves the Life He gives.

It is also very important to realise that this water represented the water that came forth from the rock that followed Israel in the wilderness, and this Rock is Christ Jesus (1 Corinthians 10:4). Remember when the Israelites were in the wilderness and there was no water, they gathered together against Moses and Aaron. And the people contended with Moses. So Moses and Aaron went to the door of the tabernacle of meeting, and they fell on their faces. And the glory of the Lord appeared to them. Then the Lord spoke to Moses, saying, "Take the rod; you and your brother Aaron gather the congregation together. Speak to the rock before their eyes, and it will yield its water; thus, you shall bring water for them out of the rock and give drink to the congregation and their animals." So, Moses took the rod from before the Lord as He commanded him. Moses and Aaron gathered the assembly together before the rock, and he said to them, "Hear now, you rebels! Must we bring water for you out of this rock?" Then Moses lifted his hand and struck the rock twice with his rod; and water came out abundantly, and the congregation and their animals drank. Then the Lord spoke to Moses and Aaron, "Because you did not believe Me, (you broke faith with Me, you acted separately from Me) and did not hallow Me, (honour Me, reveal My glory) in the eyes of the children of Israel, therefore you shall not bring this assembly into the land which I have given them." This was the water of Meribah, because the children of Israel contended with the Lord, and He was hallowed among them (Numbers 20:2-13).

God was hallowed, He was glorified and exalted in the eyes of the people, but not in the way that represents Him. The spirit in which Moses brought forth water to quench the thirst of the people was a spirit of wrath and condemnation. He therefore did not impart the faith in God we see that Jesus gives.

Moses did not reveal the grace and truth we see in Jesus for his face was not radiant with God's grace, as he struck the rock in anger. His anger at the people's thirst caused Moses to err in judgment, as the Lord had told him to *speak* to the rock, not to strike it, and therefore he failed to show them the way to the Father through faith in His Word.

One thing which demonstrates that someone is Christ's Apostle is that when they speak God's Word, those who hear, receive faith in Jesus and are filled with the Holy Spirit. Earlier in his ministry, when Moses encountered the same thirst in the people, God did tell him to strike the rock (Exodus 17:6). This represented Jesus suffering God's wrath for our sins on the cross. But this, Jesus did only once, for all time and for all people. "Jesus endured the suffering that should have been ours, the pain that we should have borne. All the while we thought that His suffering was punishment sent by God. But because of our sins He was wounded, beaten because of the evil we did. We are all healed by the punishment He suffered and made whole by the blows He received. All of us were like sheep that were lost, each of us going his own way. But the Lord made the punishment fall on Him, the punishment all of us deserved" (Isaiah 53:4-6 TEV).

God called Moses to foreshadow what He would do for us in Jesus (Hebrews 3:5). This is why at this second time when the people were thirsty, God told Moses to *speak* to the rock so that the Life-giving waters might flow freely, and all might be given eyes to see, through faith in His Word, that God's grace is sufficient to quench their thirst for Life, love and every good gift that comes from above.

Moses' face was supposed to be radiant with God's mercy, grace, longsuffering, goodness and truth when he spoke to the rock, for the Lord had showed him His face in Exodus 34:6 when He commanded Moses how to bless His people. The Lord told him saying: "This is the way you shall bless the children of Israel. Say to them: 'The Lord bless you and keep you; The Lord make His face shine upon you and be gracious to you; The Lord lift up His countenance upon you and give you peace.' So, they shall put My name on the children of Israel, and I will bless them" (Numbers 6:23-27).

Now can you see what Jesus is showing you by sending the blind man to wash in the Pool of Siloam? Oh, how the Lord Jesus longs to open your eyes through faith when you look at others, especially those who suffer with their own weak human nature and are so thirsty for Living water.

Jesus Leads us into the Promised Rest

Saying all this about Moses, I must tell you how much I love him whom God made so beautifully humble and meek; with whom He spoke face-to-face, enabling him to show us so much, at such a high cost to himself - not least that he was not allowed to lead the people into the promised rest. There is not enough room in this book to show you the significance of all this; and how through the law which came through Moses no one is made perfect, because through it we come under God's wrath, as the law exposes the sin-nature in us, which is why it was not given to Moses to lead us into the promised rest. However, I am so pleased to see Moses standing on the Mount of Transfiguration together with Elijah (the two men representing the Law and the Prophets) to support Jesus, to whom it was given before creation - through the sacrifice of Himself as the Lamb of God who takes away the sin of the world - to lead all who receive Him into the promised rest of the blessed presence of the Father.

What God told Moses to do is what we see fulfilled in Jesus. Jesus demonstrates the spirit of faith working through love when He quenched our thirst. When the Father saw His Son's love for us - as Jesus suffered the pain of our thirst, our weaknesses, our iniquities and sins - it was like sweet perfume - an acceptable, well-pleasing sacrifice to Him - for by the virtue of His Eternal Spirit (that is, His own pre-existent divine personality), Jesus offered Himself as an unblemished sacrifice to God. This is why this sacrifice of Himself never needs to be repeated, for it is perfectly sufficient for all people and for all eternity, to quench our thirst by filling us all with all of Himself.

Through the knowledge of Himself, which He Himself possesses, imparts and maintains in us, Jesus has opened the new Life-giving Way into the rest of the blessed presence of the Father. Can you see why Jesus said, "I am the Way, the Truth, and the Life. No one comes to the Father except through Me?" (John 14:6). This is why I believe one of the greatest Scriptures to show you how to judge by the Spirit is found in Isaiah 53:11, where it says, "He (Jesus) shall see [the fruit] of the travail of His soul and be satisfied; by His knowledge of Himself [which He possesses and imparts to others] shall My [uncompromisingly] righteous One, My Servant, justify many and make many righteous (upright and in right standing with God), for He shall bear their iniquities and their guilt [with the consequences, says the Lord]" (Isaiah 53:11 AMPC).

There is no true Apostle without this grace you see in Jesus being the first, middle and end of his ministry. The Life of Christ's Apostle must stand in reference to Christ's incarnation, His accomplished work on the cross, His death, His resurrection and glory at the Father's right hand. Christ's Apostles are given the priceless privilege to minister the reward of the sufferings of Jesus, which is to remove every charge and end all judgment by taking away the power of sin through the Life-giving Spirit of the new covenant.

As one of my favourite hymn states so beautifully, "Jesus paid it all, all to Him I owe, sin had left a crimson stain, He washed me white as snow." The power of Christ's Apostle is in the grace of our Lord Jesus Christ to hold back judgment, disarm satan, and set captives free from sin by giving them new Life. How wonderful to be empowered to minister the fulfilment of God's promises in Jesus. As it is written, "He will again have compassion on us, and will subdue our iniquities. You will cast all our sins into the depths of the sea" (Micah 7:19).

Washing our Spiritual Eyes

Now let me say this again so that it deeply penetrates your heart. The Spirit by which you see others must be the Spirit of Jesus Christ, for only He is the judge of the living and the dead. Only by His Spirit, by which He suffered so patiently, quietly and sweetly - giving Himself to God a perfect sacrifice - will you have the power to remove sins and end all judgment.

I pray that you will meditate on this most important Apostolic grace; for it is the Father who forms in Christ's Apostles this grace, this love, this Spirit of Life in Christ, to enable them to speak His Life-giving Word, giving faith in Jesus - who is the Rock from whom the Holy Spirit flows - to quench our thirst both now and forever. Jesus said, "Most assuredly, I say to you, he who hears My Word and believes in Him who sent Me has everlasting Life, and shall not come into judgment, but has passed from death into Life, for as the living Father sent Me, and I live because of the Father, so he who feeds on Me will live because of Me" (John 5:24, 6:57).

The reason people are so blind to their ungodly behaviour and can't stop sinning is because they don't know Jesus (1 John 3:5-9)! John shows us that if we want to help people to stop sinning, we must reveal Jesus and impart His Life-giving Spirit, for when they know Jesus who cannot sin, neither will they. Only by abiding in Him and He in us can we live free from sin and bear the fruit of His heavenly, holy, sinless Life. Jesus said that when the Father sees the fruit of His indwelling Life and Word in us, He is well pleased (John 15:7-8).

Oh how the Father longs for you to see what Jesus is showing you by sending the blind man to the Pool of Siloam, who when he washed received his sight. Jesus desires to open our spiritual eyes and help us understand what happens in all who receive His Life-giving Spirit. For this is the work of Christ's Apostles - to open people's eyes by revealing Jesus in the power of His Life-giving Spirit, so they may receive faith, forgiveness and become heirs of His Eternal Life of Sonship.

Seeing what the Father is showing you

Perhaps I may share with you about one occasion when Jesus taught me how to judge by His Spirit. It was when I laid my hands on someone in prayer. In a moment's time, the Holy Spirit showed me the layers of this individual's natural struggles. While He showed me this, I had the sense that what I saw was something I was not to look at. The next moment, He showed me this individual's spirit crying, "Save me Jesus! Save me!" Then I felt the joy of the Lord and said, "I see your spirit crying, 'Save me Jesus'!" The moment I said this, the Spirit of the Lord Jesus filled this person and instantly all the human struggles were gone. This is what it is like to give Living water to a thirsty soul.

This is an example of what it means to open people's spiritual eyes to see the goodness of the Lord Jesus in the land of the living.

In John, we read how Jesus opened the eyes of a woman who had suffered many failed marriages and was now living in a wrong relationship. What I want you to see is that He didn't judge by what He saw and heard but gave her to drink from the Living water of His Spirit.

When Jesus rested from His journey at Jacob's well in Samaria, while His disciples were in town to buy food, a woman came to draw water. Jesus asked her for some water. She said, "How is it that You, being a Jew, ask a drink from me, a Samaritan woman?" For Jews have no dealings with Samaritans. Jesus answered and said to her, "If you knew the gift God has for you, and who I am who says to you, 'Give Me a drink,' you would ask Me, and I would give you Living water." The woman said to Him, "Sir, You have nothing to draw with, and the well is deep. Where then do You get this Living water?" Jesus answered and said to her, "Whoever drinks of this water will thirst again, but whoever drinks of the water that I shall give him will never thirst. But the water that I shall give him will become in him a fountain of water springing up into everlasting Life."

The woman said to Him, "Sir, give me this water, that I may not thirst, nor come here to draw." It is obvious Jesus was talking about the Life He would give her by His Spirit, but she was still thinking of the effort she had to make to draw from this natural well. Can you see that her eyes were spiritually blind as she could not understand what Jesus was saying? So Jesus said to her, "Go, call your husband, and come here." The woman answered and said, "I have no husband." Jesus said to her, "You have well said, 'I have no husband,' for you have had five husbands, and the one whom you now have is not your husband; in that you spoke truly." It is interesting to see how when we are confronted with the truth in the way we are living how this can make us feel uncomfortable. For from the moment Jesus showed that He knew all about her, she tried to change the subject and said, "Well, you Jews think we must worship in Jerusalem, but we Samaritans think it is on this mountain."

I love to see how her fear and defensiveness did not distract Jesus. Jesus responded by saying, "It is true salvation comes by what God has accomplished through the Jews and you don't know who you worship, but I can tell you this, that the hour is coming, and now is, when you will neither on this mountain, nor in Jerusalem, worship the Father, for the true worshipers will worship the Father in spirit and truth; for the Father is seeking such to worship Him. God is Spirit, and those who worship Him must worship in spirit and truth."

You can see Jesus opened this woman's eyes, for she said to Jesus, "I know that the Messiah is coming" (who is called Christ). "When He comes, He will tell us all things." Jesus said to her, "I who speak to you am He" (John 4:7-26). Oh, how wonderful to see her spiritual eyes opened when she drank from the Life Jesus gave, for she then went to evangelise her town so that they all came to Jesus and said to the woman, "Now we believe, not because of what you said, for we ourselves have heard Him and we know that this is indeed the Christ, the Saviour of the world" (John 4:42).

Can you see the grace by which Jesus judged those who were obviously falling short of God's glory? Jesus did not condemn this woman for the failure she had suffered, but gave her a new beginning by giving her to drink of His Life-giving Spirit. For Jesus, to see God give this woman His Life was true nourishment from heaven. In other words, when Jesus felt the Life He has with the Father in heaven flow through His flesh, this fed, nourished and refreshed Him.

His Apostles did not yet know this Life, this grace, this love they were called to minister. Jesus was teaching them, as He is teaching you and me today, how to feed on Him and live because of Him (John 6:57).

Selah.
Take a moment and worshipfully meditate on this and the Holy Spirit will refresh you in your union with the Father and the Son, who is Jesus Christ our Lord.

Chapter 14

GROWING IN GRACE

Oh, how Jesus longs for all His Apostles to grow in His grace and learn from Him how to *absorb*, *disarm*, and *empower*. The deeper your roots grow into Jesus Himself, as you daily draw your nourishment for life and ministry from your union with Him, the greater His grip of grace and truth will be on your heart and mind. Jesus wants to empower you to possess His self-sacrificial love in such a measure that the devil cannot provoke you through the weaknesses, shortcomings, and failures of others to do his evil destructive work. I charge you, by the love of the Lord Jesus, to know by His Spirit in you that the devil has no claim on you, that he has nothing in common with you, that there is nothing in you that belongs to him, and that he has no power over you! Through His self-sacrificial love, Jesus enables you to *absorb* - which means you have His power to take within yourself the offensiveness of the weaknesses and failures of others and make the offence of no effect, rendering it powerless by letting it die in you; thereby you are *disarming* the devil from being able to accuse them.

You see, through guilt and condemnation the devil holds people in bondage so that they keep repeating the same mistakes. But praise God for Jesus, who has not only called us to suffer with Him the pain of other people's sins, but as we learn to suffer pain like Him (Isaiah 53; Philippians 3:10), He grants us to share the Spirit of His grace and glory so that we become ministers of the new covenant, ministers of the more excellent ministry of Jesus. This means that we have His power and love to take away every offence, fully clear the record and remove every charge, ending all judgement by freely forgiving. And most wonderful of all, we are given the privilege of *empowering* them with His Life-giving Spirit to live even as He lives.

I pray as you read this that the love of Jesus stirs your heart, for He is moved with compassion for the multitudes because they are weary and scattered. Their problems are so great that they don't know where to go for help; they are like sheep without a shepherd. Jesus is calling you today. He says, "The harvest truly is plentiful, but the labourers are few. Therefore, pray the Lord of the harvest to send you out into His harvest" (Matthew 9:35-38).

Absorb, Disarm and Empower

I use words such as *absorb*, *disarm* and *empower* because without this ability of Jesus, like Moses who in his wrath failed in judgment, Christ's Apostles won't be able to give the kind of faith in God that we see Jesus gives. God shows that without the grace and truth Jesus gives, we are not able to lead people into the promised rest of His blessed presence. I therefore encourage you to seek the same heart and mind you see in Jesus. Take a moment to mediate on the following from Philippians 2:6, so that the Holy Spirit can enlarge your heart with the love of the Father that is so perfectly revealed in Jesus: "Jesus, being in the form of God, did not consider His equality with the Father to be used to advance Himself but rather to humbly give Himself."

Jesus gave Himself, perfectly displaying the Eternal Spirit by which He came forth from the Father. And by the power of His Eternal Spirit, He took the whole Law we were unable to obey because of the weakness of the flesh, and nailed it to the cross (remember Jesus is the Word; He is the embodiment of the Law). Thereby He *absorbed* all our sins in His body as He sweetly, patiently, and quietly bore the chastisement and punishment of God's wrath that was due to us, so that He might establish the cleansing of all our sins in His own blood and fully clear our record, remove every charge, and end all judgment.

As it is written, how much more shall the blood of Christ, who through the Eternal Spirit offered Himself without spot to God, cleanse your conscience from dead works to serve the living God? (Hebrews 9:14).

By this, Jesus completely *disarmed* satan, made a public spectacle of him as He triumphed over him. For Jesus took away satan's power to accuse you of sin and keep you in bondage to fear of judgment in death. Jesus said, "Most assuredly, I say to you, he who hears My Word and believes in Him who sent Me has everlasting Life, and shall not come into judgment, but has passed from death into Life" (John 5:24). What Jesus is saying to those whose hearts and minds are spiritually made alive by Him is this: "The reason you can hear Me speaking God's Word is because His Life is in you, and if His Life is in you this means you are no longer under His judgment but have already passed from death into Life."

Now that Jesus has all authority in heaven, on earth and under the earth, He can empower you continuously and forever with His Life at the Father's right hand. Jesus said, "Because I live, you will live also, you will know that I am in My Father, and you in Me, and I in you. As the living Father sent Me, and I live because of the Father, so he who feeds on Me will live because of Me" (John 14:19-20, 6:57).

I pray that you may know through experience for yourself that Jesus, who is your Life, will never fail to do the Father's will by continually filling and flooding you with His Eternal Life of Sonship, His Life of perfect righteousness, peace, and joy in the presence of the Father. For out of His fullness (abundance) we have all received [all had a share and we were all supplied with] one grace after another and spiritual blessing upon spiritual blessing and even favour upon favour and gift [heaped] upon gift (John 1:16 AMPC).

Now, can you see that you have the witness the Father has given of His Son Jesus living in your heart? And oh, how gloriously powerful is this witness that we now have Eternal Life in Him (1 John 5:10). This means you have the Anointing of Jesus the Holy One, the Anointing of the new creation, the power of the age to come, this heavenly treasure in your earthen vessel, so that, like Jesus, you are a living expression of the grace and truth of the Father.

Jesus prayed, "Father, I have given them the glory You gave Me - the glorious unity of being one, as we are, I in them and You in Me, all being perfected into one - so that the world will know You sent Me and will understand that You love them as much as You love Me. Father, I want them with Me - these You've given Me - so that they can see My glory. You gave Me the glory because You loved Me before the world began! O righteous Father, the world doesn't know You, but I do; and these disciples know You sent Me, because I have revealed You to them and I will keep on revealing You so that the mighty love You have for Me may be in them, and I in them" (John 17:22-26 TLB).

The Greater Works

While reading this you can see Jesus doing the greater works in His High Priestly work at the Father's right hand. The reason you are shown this by the Holy Spirit is so that you can see what the Father has given you in Jesus. You see, Jesus keeps you from the evil one in this world simply by revealing the Father in you, so that the unbroken fellowship He enjoys in the intimate presence of the Father lives in you and so that you might enjoy the same love with which He is loved.

Now, I want you to hear Jesus praying for you - Jesus prays, "And [now] I am no more in the world, but these are [still] in the world, and I am coming to You. Holy Father, keep in Your Name ['in the knowledge of Yourself'] those whom You have given Me, that they may be one as We [are one]. While I was with them, I kept and preserved them in Your Name ['in the knowledge and worship of You']. Those You have given Me I guarded and protected, and not one of them has perished" (John 17:11-12 AMPC).

The wonder of the Father's love for Jesus and His unbroken intimacy with Him overwhelms me and keeps me inwardly knowing, perceiving, and recognising the Father so that the evil one, and all the things of this world, have nothing in me. It is glorious beyond measure, that we are not only given to live in the greater works Jesus is now doing as our great High Priest-King at the Father's right hand, but that we also are given the priceless privilege to give this to those entrusted to us, so that they too may share the fellowship we have with the Father and His Son Jesus. This fellowship with the Father and His Son Jesus is the distinguishing mark of Christians all over the earth and in heaven!

When you read the writings of John you know this is not the work of a mere man because each word is full of the breath of God and gives Life to all who believe in His Son. John writes, "No man has ever seen God at any time; the only unique Son, or the only begotten God, Who is in the bosom [in the intimate presence] of the Father, He has declared Him [He has revealed Him and brought Him out where He can be seen; He has interpreted Him and He has made Him known]. And we [actually] saw His glory (His honour, His majesty), such glory as an only begotten son receives from his father, full of grace (favour, loving-kindness) and truth" (John 1:18, 14 AMPC).

John's credentials as an Apostle of Christ are unmistakably clear, for he does not represent himself but presents Jesus as he writes under the inspiration of His Spirit. John says, "The One who existed from the beginning is the One we have heard and seen. We saw Him with our own eyes and touched Him with our own hands. He is Jesus Christ, the Word of Life. This One who is Life from God was shown to us, and we have seen Him. And now we testify and announce to you that He is the One who is Eternal Life. He was with the Father, and then He was shown to us. We are telling you about what we ourselves have actually seen and heard, so that you may have fellowship with us. And our fellowship is with the Father and with His Son, Jesus Christ" (1 John 1:1-3 NLT).

Found Faithful

Whatever place God gave Christ's Apostles in their short earthly lives, the greatest reward awaited them in heaven. Remember Jesus said, "Assuredly I say to you, that in the regeneration, when the Son of Man sits on the throne of His glory, you who have followed Me will also sit on twelve thrones, judging the twelve tribes of Israel" (Matthew 19:28). What is most important in the kingdom of God is that we are all found faithful in the place God has given us and do the work He has entrusted to us. When Jesus was about to leave earth to return to the Father He said, "Father I have glorified You on the earth. I have finished the work which You have given Me to do" (John 17:4). As it is written, "Jesus ... was faithful to Him who appointed Him" (Hebrews 3:2).

I love to see the humble and meek heart of Jesus in John, that he was willing to drink the cup of His suffering and pay the price to bring us such glorious riches from His presence.

According to a church father, Tertullian, John was cast into burning oil before a large crowd in the Roman Colosseum to stop him from making Jesus known. But the work the Father had given John was not finished yet, so, to the amazement of the crowd, John came out of the burning oil unharmed - which caused many to receive Jesus as Lord. After this, John was banished to Patmos where he wrote the Book of the Revelation of Jesus Christ. Now John has gone before us and has entered his reward; he is sitting alongside Jesus on His throne in the kingdom. Remember Jesus said, "To him who overcomes, I will grant to sit with Me on My throne, as I also overcame and sat down with My Father on His throne" (Revelation 3:21).

In all the works Jesus gave John - not least his writing, under the inspiration of the Holy Spirit, the Gospel of John, the three epistles and the Book of Revelation - John shows the greater works that Jesus as our Apostle, Great High Priest and King is doing at the Father's right hand in heaven, the works He is willing to entrust to His Apostles today, by granting them to make them known in the power of the Holy Spirit to this generation.

Remember Jesus said, "Most assuredly, I say to you, he who believes in Me, the works that I do he will do also; and greater works than these he will do, because I go to My Father. And whatever you ask in My name (representing Me before the Father), that I will do, that the Father may be glorified in the Son. If you ask anything in My name, I will do it" (John 14:12-14).

Selah.
Take a moment and worshipfully meditate on this and the Holy Spirit will refresh you in your union with the Father and the Son, who is Jesus Christ our Lord.

Chapter 15

SEEING CHRIST GLORIFIED

There is so much more I would love to say about John, but before I move on to Paul, perhaps I may close this part of the book with this thought: that John was given the great privilege of seeing Jesus not only in His resurrected body, shortly after His Resurrection, and then for nearly forty days until His Ascension; but he was also given the extraordinary privilege of seeing Jesus in His glorified body. This happened when he received heavenly visions of Jesus - visions that are contained within the Book of Revelation.

His Resurrected Body

First, I want you to see Jesus Christ as He reveals Himself as the Son of Man in His resurrected body. In Luke 24, we see Jesus appear in His resurrected body, which according to Scripture had seen no corruption in death. Jesus showed His wounds as proof that He was the One who suffered and died but now, according to Scripture, is alive. Jesus ate some fish and honey in their presence to show He was not just a spirit but had flesh and bones. Then He said to them, "These are the words which I spoke to you while I was still with you, that all things must be fulfilled which were written in the Law of Moses and the Prophets and the Psalms concerning Me." And He opened their understanding, that they might comprehend the Scriptures.

Remember I showed you this when I wrote about Peter - that Christ's Apostles are enabled to make Jesus known in the power of the Holy Spirit by opening the Scriptures. So consider this, that even while the disciples could see Jesus in His resurrected body, they did not believe until He opened the Scriptures to them. Always remember that it is through Jesus the Scriptures are opened to you and that the Scriptures testify about Him.

Then He said to them, "Thus it is written, and thus it was necessary for the Christ to suffer and to rise from the dead the third day, and that repentance and remission of sins should be preached in His name to all nations, beginning at Jerusalem. And you are witnesses of these things. Behold, I send the Promise of My Father upon you; but tarry in the city of Jerusalem until you are endued with power from on high." Now when He had spoken these things, while they watched, He was taken up, and a cloud received Him out of their sight. And while they looked steadfastly toward heaven as He went up, behold, two men stood by them in white apparel, who also said, "Men of Galilee, why do you stand gazing up into heaven? This same Jesus, who was taken up from you into heaven, will so come in like manner as you saw Him go into heaven" (Luke 24:39-49; Acts 1:9-11).

When Daniel foresaw this happening, a long time before, he said; "I was watching in the night visions, and behold, one like the Son of Man, Coming with the clouds of heaven! He came to the Ancient of Days, and they brought Him near before Him. Then to Him was given dominion and glory and a kingdom, that all peoples, nations, and languages should serve Him. His dominion is an everlasting dominion, which shall not pass away, and His kingdom the one which shall not be destroyed" (Daniel 7:13-14).

What I would like you to see is that there is a difference between the resurrected body of Jesus and His glorified body. I say this to help you believe that God is a rewarder of those who diligently seek Him, and that He has the power to strengthen, complete, perfect, make you what you ought to be, and equip you with everything good that you may carry out His perfect will; while He Himself works in you and accomplishes that which is pleasing in His sight, through Jesus Christ; to Whom be the glory forever and ever, Amen. (Hebrews 11:6, 13:21)

His Glorified Body

Now look at Jesus as He reveals Himself in His glorified body; for when you see Him in His glorified body you will see the reward of the Lord you are called to share as a co-heir with Him (Romans 8:17). I pray therefore that you keep your eyes fixed on Jesus, who is your Life and who gives and maintains His Life in you, while you serve Him and eagerly await His return.

"The Book of the Revelation of Jesus Christ, which God gave Him to show His servants, contain things which must shortly take place. And He sent and signified it by His angel to His servant John, who bore witness to the Word of God, and to the testimony of Jesus Christ, to all things that he saw. Blessed is he who reads and those who hear the words of this prophecy and keep those things which are written in it; for the time is near. Grace to you and peace from Him who is and who was and who is to come, and from the seven Spirits who are before His throne, and from Jesus Christ, the faithful witness, the firstborn from the dead, and the ruler over the kings of the earth. To Him who loved us and washed us from our sins in His own blood and has made us kings and priests to His God and Father, to Him be glory and dominion forever and ever. Amen. Behold, He is coming with clouds, and every eye will see Him, even they who pierced Him. And all the tribes of the earth will mourn because of Him. Even so, Amen. "I am the Alpha and the Omega, the Beginning and the End," says the Lord, "who is and who was and who is to come, the Almighty" (Revelation 1:1-8).

May we all follow John's example to live in the Spirit each day, so that the Holy Spirit can help us to see, hear and perceive what is freely given to us in Jesus; for He who loves us longs to share with us the glory He has with the Father in heaven.

Now John saw the reward of the Lord Jesus, the Son of Man, for he saw Jesus in His glorified body. John says, "I was in the Spirit on the Lord's Day, and I heard behind me a loud voice, as of a trumpet then I turned to see the voice that spoke with me. And having turned I saw One like the Son of Man, clothed with a garment down to the feet and girded about the chest with a golden band. His head and hair were white like wool, as white as snow, and His eyes like a flame of fire; His feet were like fine brass, as if refined in a furnace, and His voice as the sound of many waters; He had in His right hand seven stars, out of His mouth went a sharp two-edged sword, and His countenance was like the sun shining in its strength. And when I saw Him, I fell at His feet as dead. But He laid His right hand on me, saying to me, "Do not be afraid; I am the First and the Last. I am He who lives, the Ever-living One, [living in the eternity of eternities] and was dead, and behold, I am alive forevermore. Amen. And I have the keys of Hades (hell) and Death" (Revelation 1:10-18 NKJ/AMPC).

Seeing Jesus in His glorified body, consider that you are co-heirs with Him of the Life He has with the Father. Therefore give Him praise each day by living in this world as He lives in heaven.

Selah.
Take a moment and worshipfully meditate on this and the Holy Spirit will refresh you in your union with the Father and the Son, who is Jesus Christ our Lord.

Part 4

PAUL, CHRIST'S APOSTLE

Chapter 16

PROCLAIMING THE LIFE-GIVING GOSPEL

When Jesus ascended to His throne at the Father's right hand, He gave some to be Apostles. Paul's Apostleship was no less given by Jesus than the other Apostles, but it was given in a different way. Peter and John had been with Jesus for many years and shared in His Life on earth. Paul had never experienced this, but what I find so beautiful to see is that he knew Jesus no less intimately; which shows you the immeasurable riches of the glory of the Father's grace by which He made Paul Christ's Apostle. I say this so that when you pray and worship the Father in the power of His Spirit and Truth, you may see Him reveal His Son in you. For to this you were predestined long before you were born. Never forget that it is the Father who longs to be merciful to you, so that He may satisfy the great love He feels for you by continuously renewing and transforming you inwardly into the image of His Son.

When Paul met Jesus, the kindness and the love of God our Saviour towards man appeared to him. And what Paul received, God gives to us all in Jesus. For it is not by our works of righteousness, but through His Mercy that He saves us, by the washing of regeneration and renewing of the Holy Spirit, whom He pours out on us abundantly through Jesus Christ our Saviour. And since we have been justified by His grace, we have become heirs with the confident expectation of Eternal Life (Titus 3:4-7 NET). I pray that these thoughts of the Holy Spirit flood your heart and cause you to lift your hands in praise to God the Father of our Lord Jesus Christ, for in Him you are made full, and having come to fullness of Life in Christ, you too are filled with the Godhead - Father, Son and Holy Spirit - and reach full spiritual stature (Colossians 2:10 AMPC). Just think about this, your calling is nothing less than the stature of the fullness of the Father that you see in Jesus (Ephesians 4:13)!

Paul said, "It pleased God, who separated me from my mother's womb to call me through His grace, so that He might reveal His Son in me, so that I might preach Him among the Gentiles" (Galatians 1:15-16). Paul received that same inward knowing from God that even before he was born, he was called and chosen to be Christ's Apostle. This does not mean that Paul had an easy journey into his calling; his road in life, while glorious, was about as rough as they come. But Paul was assured and knew that God always works all things together for good for those who love Him and are called according to His purpose. (Romans 8:28).

I say this to encourage you that even if you feel that your journey into the calling upon your life seems challenging in many ways, and even if you feel that you don't fit the narrative of Peter and John's calling because you did not walk with Jesus like they did, then perhaps Paul's example will encourage you to see that the grace of God is more than sufficient to work in you what you see in them.

When Paul talked about himself being Christ's Apostle he said, "I am the least of all the Apostles. I do not even deserve to be called an Apostle, because I persecuted God's church. But by God's grace I am what I am, and the grace that He gave me was not without effect. On the contrary, I have worked harder than any of the other Apostles, although it was not really my own doing, but God's grace working with me" (1 Corinthians 15:9-11 TEV).

When Jesus called Paul He said, in the Hebrew language, "Saul, Saul, why are you persecuting Me? It is hard for you to kick against the goads." The goad is a long stick with a sharp metal point used to prod oxen into action. In other words, Jesus had been prodding Paul for some time, but Paul had hardened his heart against Him.

Paul said, "Who are You, Lord?" He said, "I am Jesus, whom you are persecuting." Trembling and astonished, Paul said, "Lord, what do You want me to do?" Jesus said, "Rise and stand on your feet; for I have appeared to you for this purpose, to make you a minister and a witness both of the things which you have seen and of the things which I will yet reveal to you. I will deliver you from the Jewish people, as well as from the Gentiles, to whom I now send you, to open their eyes, in order to turn them from darkness to light, and from the power of satan to God, that they may receive forgiveness of sins and an inheritance among those who are sanctified by faith in Me" (Acts 9:4-6, 26:14-18).

You can clearly see in Paul how he grew in the riches of God's grace through the knowledge of the Lord Jesus and how the Life-giving message of Jesus was formed in him. Paul never lost sight of the vision of Jesus in his heart. For him the Gospel was clear to see. He said, "I make known to you, brethren, that the Gospel which was preached by me is not according to man. For I neither received it from man, nor was I taught it, but it came through the revelation of Jesus Christ" (Galatians 1:11-12).

The Gospel by the Revelation of Jesus

As with all Christ's Apostles, the Gospel Paul preached showed that he was truly an Apostle of Jesus Christ by the will of God. Paul opened all his letters with a statement like this: "Paul, an Apostle of Jesus Christ by the will of God, separated to the Gospel of God" (Ephesians 1:1; Romans 1:1). He said, "I was not disobedient to the heavenly vision (the vision of Jesus), but declared first to those in Damascus and in Jerusalem, and throughout all the region of Judea, and then to the Gentiles, that they should repent, turn to God, and do works befitting repentance. For these reasons the Jews seized me in the temple and tried to kill me. Therefore, having obtained help from God, to this day I stand, witnessing both to small and great, saying no other things than those which the prophets and Moses said would come - that the Christ would suffer, that He would be the first to rise from the dead, and would proclaim light to the Jewish people and to the Gentiles" (Acts 26:19-23).

No matter what challenges the church faced, the answer for Paul was always alive, available, and all-powerful; for Jesus is the same, yesterday, today, and forever. Jesus is *the power of the Gospel*. His righteousness is received and enjoyed in no other way than simply by faith in Him, for it is the Father who made Jesus our righteousness. In other words, Jesus is upholding you with His own righteousness. The righteousness He enjoys with the Father is what He imparts and maintains in you by His Spirit. There is absolutely no other means of obtaining freedom from sin and perfect peace with God other than through the perfect righteousness you receive by faith in Jesus.

The Gospel that Christ's Apostles proclaimed in the power of the heaven-sent Holy Spirit came through the revelation of Jesus in them, as Paul so powerfully explains: "Whatever former things I had that might have been gain to me, I have come to consider as [one combined] loss for Christ's sake. Yes, furthermore, I count everything as loss compared to the possession of the priceless privilege (the overwhelming preciousness, the surpassing worth, and supreme advantage) of knowing Christ Jesus my Lord and of progressively becoming more deeply and intimately acquainted with Him [of perceiving and recognizing and understanding

Him more fully and clearly]. For His sake I have lost everything and consider it all to be mere rubbish (refuse, dregs), in order that I may win (gain) Christ (the Anointed One), and that I may [actually] be found and known as in Him, not having any [self-achieved] righteousness that can be called my own, based on my obedience to the Law's demands (ritualistic uprightness and supposed right standing with God thus acquired), but possessing that [genuine righteousness] which comes through faith in Christ (the Anointed One), the [truly] right standing with God, which comes from God by [saving] faith. [For my determined purpose is] that I may know Him [that I may progressively become more deeply and intimately acquainted with Him, perceiving and recognizing and understanding the wonders of His Person more strongly and more clearly], and that I may in that same way come to know the power outflowing from His resurrection [which it exerts over believers], and that I may so share His sufferings as to be continually transformed [in spirit into His likeness even] to His death, [in the hope] that if possible I may attain to the [spiritual and moral] resurrection [that lifts me] out from among the dead [even while in the body]" (Philippians 3:7-11 AMPC).

I trust you can see from the above scripture that the Gospel Paul preached was the Spirit of Christ's Life in him - not in mere knowledge that can be taught by man, but by the revelation of Christ's Life in him - a Life of Sonship in perfect righteousness, peace and joy with the Father.

The True Gospel has Immense Power

A wonderful Apostle of Christ called Edward McKendree Bounds, born in 1835 and passed on to glory in 1913, wrote an amazing book called *Power through Prayer*. In it he said, "It takes twenty years to make the sermon, for it takes twenty years to make the person. The Church is looking for better methods; God is looking for better men." Paul was such a man in whom God could form His Gospel. Because of Christ in him Paul could say, "For as much as is in me, I am ready to preach the Gospel to you" (Romans 1:15). As I write this, the Life of Jesus wells up in me with His Word. I therefore pray, together with the Apostle Paul, that Christ may be continually formed in you by His Spirit so that He is the Life you live and the Gospel you preach (Galatians 4:19).

When young Timothy was being challenged in the church by the weaknesses and failures of people's human nature, and by a power struggle from those who were not Apostles - who were not sent by Jesus, but came with a different Gospel that demanded submission to the old covenant methods of the law instead of faith in Jesus as the means of being blessed and enjoying freedom from sin and righteousness with God - Paul encouraged Timothy to look at the good work Jesus had begun in him, by simply believing in Him giving him a new Life in perfect righteousness, peace and joy through the Holy Spirit.

Paul writes to Timothy, "I am so thankful to Jesus our Lord for choosing me as one of His representatives and giving me the strength to be faithful to Him, even though I used to scoff at the name of Jesus. I hunted down His people, harming them in every way I could. But God had mercy on me because I didn't know what I was doing, for I didn't know Jesus at that time. Oh, how kind our Lord was, for he showed me how to trust Him and become full of the love of Jesus!" Paul says, "The grace of God was exceedingly great towards me as He had faith in me and filled me with His faith and He loved me, filling me with His love through Jesus. How true it is, and how I long that everyone should know it, that Jesus came into the world to save sinners - because I was the greatest of them all. But God had mercy on me so that Jesus could use me as an example to show everyone how patient He is with even the worst sinners, so that others will realise that they, too, can have everlasting Life (1 Timothy 1:12-17 TLB/NKJV).

Every Gospel that is preached will be tested whether it truly comes from the throne of grace by the power it has when confronted by the weak human nature. Only the true Gospel has the power to save to the uttermost, for only the true Gospel has the all-powerful Life-giving Spirit of the ever-living intercession of Jesus to not only free you from sin, but to keep you free to enjoy His holy, acceptable and well-pleasing Life with the Father. So, let me say this again that it may deeply penetrate your heart: all Christ's Apostles are identified as being truly sent to represent Jesus Christ by the Gospel they preach! As for Paul, the Gospel was alive in him. He said, "I am not ashamed of the Gospel of Christ, for it is the power of God unto salvation for everyone who believes, for the Jew first and also for the Greek. For in it the righteousness of God is revealed from faith to faith; as it is written, 'The just shall live by faith'" (Romans 1:16-17). Paul proclaimed the Gospel, for he knew that through it God's power is revealed unto salvation. He knew that everyone who received faith in Jesus by hearing the Word of God was given righteousness, peace, and joy with God by His Spirit.

God-given Ability to Speak His Word

One of the greatest privileges of being Christ's Apostle is to have the power of Jesus Christ to preach, proclaim, make known and unveil the Gospel - to demonstrate His Life-giving Spirit and give it freely to live in all who receive Him. This is a great privilege. As the scripture shows, angels longed to look into these things and to see God in the flesh.

Kings and prophets desired to know the grace and truth that has come to us in Jesus; for He is the mystery of the Gospel, the Life He ever lives to give, to live in us, is the ever-living hope of glory (1 Peter 1:12; 1 Timothy 3:16; Luke 10:24, 8:10; Colossians 1:27-29).

Now who is qualified for this? Who is sufficient in ability to preach the Gospel? When God called Moses - who struggled with his inability to speak, especially in the face of confrontation, having been broken into a meek, lowly and humble man over many years of trial and self-denial - God said, "Who has made man's mouth? Have not I, the Lord? Now therefore, go, and I will be with your mouth and teach you what you shall say" (Exodus 4:11-12). Moses learned to speak the words of God by the Spirit of God, and thereby he saw Him fulfil His promise, to the glory of His name.

Moses also understood by the Spirit, that God would raise up someone like him in the future. Speaking about Jesus, he said, "I will put My words in His mouth and He shall speak all that I command Him... Him you shall hear" (Deuteronomy 18:18, 15). John the Baptist said about Jesus, "The One Whom God has sent speaks God's words, because God gives Him the fullness of His Spirit. The Father loves His Son and has put everything in His power" (John 3:34-35 TEV). Jesus said, "Most assuredly I say to you, the Son can do nothing of Himself. The words that I speak to you I do not speak on My own authority; but the Father who dwells in Me does the works" (John 5:19, 14:10).

All Christ's Apostles understand deep within the inclination of their hearts, that their ability to preach the Gospel is not from themselves but from what God works through them. As Paul says, "We are Christ's ambassadors, and God is using us to speak to you. We urge you, as though Christ himself is pleading with you, 'Be reconciled to God'!" (2 Corinthians 5:20 NLT). You can clearly see how the

Father was working with Paul because when he began to tell others about Jesus, God anointed him with the Holy Spirit and with power. And by the divine influence of His Spirit the Father drew everyone to Jesus, so that through Jesus they might receive a warm welcome in His presence (2 Corinthians 6:1-2 AMPC). This Divine influence - this drawing, this unction, this anointing - comes from the Spirit of the Father and is a sure mark in the lives of all Christ's Apostles! Jesus said, "No one can come to Me unless the Father who sent Me draws him; and I will raise him up at the last day. It is written in the prophets, 'And they shall all be taught by God.' Therefore, everyone who has heard and learned from the Father comes to Me" (John 6:44-45).

Oh, how I long to imprint this deep within your heart, so that you might yearn together with the Holy Spirit that Christ, the ever-Living Word, be formed in you afresh each day to enable you to speak by His Spirit His Life-giving Word.

Paul says, "Not that we are fit (qualified and sufficient in ability) of ourselves to form personal judgments or to claim or count anything as coming from us, but our power and ability and sufficiency are from God." In simple terms Paul says, "I would never dare think anything comes from myself for my ability is what God works through me. [It is He] Who has qualified us [making us to be fit and worthy and sufficient] as ministers and dispensers of a new covenant [of salvation through Christ], not [ministers] of the letter (of legally written code) but of the Spirit; for the code [of the Law] kills, but the [Holy] Spirit makes alive" (2 Corinthians 3:5-6 AMPC). Paul says, "As it is written: 'Eye has not seen, nor ear heard, nor have entered into the heart of man the things which God has prepared for those who love Him.' But God has revealed them to us through His Spirit. These things we also speak, not in words which man's wisdom teaches but which the Holy Spirit teaches. People who aren't spiritual can't receive these truths from God's Spirit. It all sounds foolish to them and they can't understand it, for only those who are spiritual can understand what the Spirit means. Those who are spiritual can evaluate all things, but they themselves cannot be evaluated by others. For, 'Who can know the Lord's thoughts? Who knows enough to teach Him?' But we understand these things, for we have the mind of Christ" (1 Corinthians 2:9-10, 13-16).

God-given Ability to Hear His Word

It is as much the work of God's Spirit for us to hear as it is to speak His Word. Jesus said, "Blessed are your ears because they hear" (Matthew 13:16). He also said, "Most assuredly, I say to you, he who hears My Word and believes in Him who sent Me has everlasting Life, and shall not come into judgment, but has passed from death into Life" (John 5:24). What Jesus is saying to those whose hearts and minds are spiritually made alive by Him is this: the reason you can hear Me speaking God's Word is because His Life is in you, and if His Life is in you this shows you are no longer under His judgment but have already passed from death into Life.

Now this is essential for you to understand as it affects the spiritual mindset with which you preach the Gospel. What do I mean by 'spiritual mindset'? Well you know that according to our natural nature we are all spiritually dead and separated from God because of the sin-nature in us. We are lost, without hope and without God in the world, but God who is rich in mercy because of the great love with which He loves us, even though we were spiritually dead, made us alive with Jesus. Through His Life-giving Spirit in us Jesus has liberated us from the dominion of sin and death. And His Life in us is the new Life-giving way to enjoy uninterrupted fellowship with the Father. Jesus shows that those who can hear Him speaking the words of God are experiencing His Life and are no longer spiritually dead, no longer separated from God - under His judgment. You see the words Jesus speaks are Spirit and Life. And through the gospel we are now given the immense privilege to speak by His Spirit His Life-giving words, so that those who hear us are made alive with Jesus and liberated from the awful dominion of sin and death. This is the new spiritual mindset with which we now preach.

I have shared with you about this grace of Christ's Apostles again and again because I pray that in all you seek in Jesus, to be gifted and enabled by Him, you seek most of all to speak by His Life-giving Spirit, so that all who hear you are fed with His Life. Knowledge is wonderful and necessary, but it puffs up with pride when the Life-giving Spirit of Jesus is lacking in the words you speak. This is why Paul always encouraged the Church to pray for him with all prayer and supplication in the Spirit. He said, "…so that utterance may be given to me, that I may open my mouth boldly to make known the mystery of the Gospel, for which I am an ambassador in chains; that I may speak boldly, as I ought to speak" (Ephesians 6:18-20). I want you to realise that it is an Apostolic grace to know inwardly that God is pleased through the message preached to save those who believe (1 Corinthians 1:18-25).

Coming Alongside Others

Paul understood that faith in Christ comes by hearing God's Word. He knew that when you believe in your heart that God raised Jesus from the dead, and confess that He is Lord, you will be saved. A powerful example of this is when Jesus, after His resurrection, drew alongside His uncle, Cleopas (the brother of Joseph), who was walking most likely with his wife Mary, some seven miles to Emmaus. They were suffering painful despair having witnessed Jesus' death on the cross. As Jesus opened the scriptures to them about Himself, beginning at Moses and all the prophets, and broke bread with them, their eyes were opened, and they knew Him. Then they said to one another, "Did not our hearts burn within us while He talked and opened the scriptures to us?" (Luke 24:32).

You can clearly see that when Jesus Christ, the ever-living Word, fills your heart, you are enabled by Him to believe unto righteousness. And according to His Spirit in you, you will begin to confess your salvation. The Scripture says, "Whoever believes on Him will not be put to shame. For there is no distinction between Jew and Greek, for the same Lord over all is rich to all who call upon Him. For 'whoever calls on the name of the Lord shall be saved.' But how shall they call on Him in whom they have not believed? And how shall they believe in Him of whom they have not heard? And how shall they hear without a preacher? And how shall they preach unless they are sent?" (Romans 10:9-15).

In other words, how would Cleopas and Mary have believed if Jesus had not come alongside them and revealed Himself to them? When I think of Jesus coming alongside them, and how He now comes alongside others with His Living presence through those who represent Him, the following scripture comes alive: "How beautiful are the feet of those who preach the Gospel of peace, who bring glad tidings of good things!" (Romans 10:15).

Tell Everyone about Jesus

One of the most important things to see in all Christ's Apostles, which you see in Paul, is that they know God desires all men to be saved. The Gospel burned with such holy fire in Paul that it compelled him to go into all the world and *tell* everyone about Jesus. Paul says, "the Gospel, which you heard, and which has been preached [as being designed for and offered without restrictions] to every person under heaven, and of which [Gospel] I, Paul, became a minister" (Colossians 1:23 AMPC). "For it is good and acceptable in the sight of God our Saviour, who desires all men to be saved and to come to the knowledge of the truth. For there is one God and one Mediator between God and men, the Man Christ Jesus, who gave Himself a ransom for all, to be testified in due time, for which I was appointed a preacher and an Apostle - I am speaking the truth in Christ and not lying - a teacher of the Gentiles in faith and truth" (1 Timothy 2:3-7).

You see, when anyone receives faith in Jesus by hearing the Gospel, they receive His Life. And when Christ's Life becomes their Life, they are no longer the same, they are a new creature, born again - born of God - children of the Living God. Paul shares how at one time he did not understand this, he did not understand what it means to be a Christian, because he mistakenly thought that Jesus was just a man, like any other man. How differently he thinks now that Jesus has come to live in his heart by His Spirit, now he knows that when anyone becomes a Christian, they become a brand-new person on the inside. The old life of sin is passed away and a new Life has come. While Christians still live in the same body, they are born of God. Having been made alive with Jesus, they are a new creation (2 Corinthians 5:15-16 TLB); "[and in this new creation all distinctions vanish.] There is no room for and there can be neither Greek nor Jew, circumcised nor uncircumcised, [nor difference between nations whether alien] barbarians or Scythians [who are the most savage of all], nor slave or free man; but Christ is all and in all [everything and everywhere, to all men, without distinction of person]" (Colossians 3:11 AMPC). In other words, Jesus is equally available to all who call upon His name. And when you have Jesus, you have all of God, for in Him dwells the fullness of God. What I want you to see is that the first and foremost commission of all Christ's Apostles is to *tell* everyone about Jesus.

Selah.

Take a moment and worshipfully meditate on this and the Holy Spirit will refresh you in your union with the Father and the Son, who is Jesus Christ our Lord.

Chapter 17

THE JOY OF THE LORD

"Looking unto Jesus, the author and finisher of our faith, who for the joy that was set before Him endured the cross, despising the shame, and has sat down at the right hand of the throne of God" (Hebrews 12:2).

The night before His death, Jesus said to His Apostles, "Therefore, you now have sorrow, but I will see you again and your heart will rejoice, and your joy no one will take from you." Then He prayed, "Father, now I am coming to You. I say these things while I am still in the world, so that My joy may be made full and complete and perfect in them [that they may experience My delight fulfilled in them, that My enjoyment may be perfected in their own souls, that they may have My gladness within them, filling their hearts]" (John 16:22 NKJV, 17:13 AMPC). The joy that Jesus is talking about, that lived in Him and enabled Him to endure the cross and despise the shame, is the same joy that He gives to live in all His Apostles, to enable them to break through every barrier that would resist the Gospel from being proclaimed. It is a true mark of Apostleship to know this joy that is inexpressible and full of glory, for we now see Jesus - He is Lord - seated at the Father's right hand in the immense reward of His labour. We preach the Gospel, the power of God unto salvation, because we share in the joy of His riches in glory.

In Paul, you can clearly see what this joy looks like when he writes from prison that we are to "Rejoice in the Lord always. And again, he says, I will say, rejoice! Let your gentleness (your unselfishness, your friendliness) be known to all men. The Lord is at hand, He is coming soon"

(Philippians 4:4). Paul says, "Now I go bound in the spirit to Jerusalem (drawn there irresistibly by the Holy Spirit, in obedience to the Holy Spirit) not knowing the things that will happen to me there, except that the Holy Spirit testifies in every city, saying that chains and tribulations await me. But none of these things move me; nor do I count my life dear to myself, so that I may finish my race with joy, and the ministry which I received from the Lord Jesus, to testify to the Gospel of the grace of God" (Acts 20:22-24). In other words, Paul says, "My Life on earth would seem meaningless unless it is spent in the joy of doing the work assigned me by the Lord Jesus - the work of telling others the Good News."

What I would like you to see is that the Lord Jesus needs His Apostles today to have this joy - or I should say this way of thinking - living deep within their hearts, so that they can break through every barrier and preach the Gospel when in their own strength they would fail to see the power of God unto salvation for all the nations.

Breaking through Barriers

Let me give you an example of what I mean by breaking through every barrier - barriers of opposition, ridicule, and intimidation. Paul says, "I plead with you - yes, I, Paul - and I plead gently, as Christ Himself would do. Yet some of you think my deeds and words are merely those of an ordinary man. Of course, it is true that I am an ordinary, weak human being, but I don't use human plans and methods to win my battles. I use God's mighty weapons, not those made by men, to knock down the devil's strongholds. These weapons can break down every proud argument against God and every wall that can be built to keep men from finding Him. With these weapons I can capture rebels and bring them back to God and change them into men whose hearts' desire is obedience to Christ. I will use these weapons against every rebel who remains after I have first used them on you yourselves and you surrender to Christ."

Paul continues, "The trouble with you is that you look at me and I seem weak and powerless, but you don't look beneath the surface. Yet if anyone can claim the power and authority of Christ, I certainly can. I may seem to be boasting more than I should about my authority over you - authority to help you, not to hurt you - but I shall make good every claim. I say this so that you will not think I am just blustering when I scold you in my letters. 'Don't bother about his letters,' some say. 'He sounds big, but it's all noise. When he gets here you will see that there is nothing great about him, and you have never heard a worse preacher!'

Paul concludes, "Oh, don't worry, I wouldn't dare say that I am as wonderful as these other men who tell you how good they are! Their trouble is that they are only measuring themselves with themselves and comparing themselves with each other, measuring themselves against their own ideas. They are without understanding of Christ in them and therefore behave unwisely" (2 Corinthians 10:1-13 TLB).

The above verses are taken from the Living Bible to help you catch what the Apostle is saying. The reason I share this is so that you can see, from what challenged Paul, how to overcome these kinds of barriers of opposition, ridicule and intimidation. Like Paul, I pray that you will see "the Life of Christ" so mightily and continuously formed in you by His Spirit that you will look to Him and Him alone, and never dare compare yourself to anyone, but that you will simply love and honour everyone.

I charge you in Christ not even to compare yourself to your own human state, no matter how weak or powerless you may feel. Do not limit the Almighty by limiting yourself. Instead stay in faith, look to Jesus, live in Him, so that you will see the fullness of His Life in you and represent Him as a true Apostle (Read Jeremiah 9:23-24).

Follow the loving heart of Jesus that you see in Paul and learn to think like him in his love for others. Paul says, "I can never stop thanking God for all the wonderful gifts He has given you. Now that you are Christ's: He has enriched your whole life. He has given you a full understanding of the truth; what I told you Christ could do for you has happened! Now you have every grace and blessing; every spiritual gift and power for doing His will are yours during this time of waiting for the return of our Lord Jesus Christ" (1 Corinthians 1:4-7 TLB).

His Power in our Weakness

Perhaps I can give you a small example from my own experience in having to overcome some barriers. In 1989, the Lord Jesus sent me to Canterbury, England to hold a 'Jesus Now' crusade. At that time I was pressed beyond measure from every side. We had no money; my wife Virginia was expecting our second son Zachary; we had no house and were living in a room in the loft of some very gracious people; and I had no co-workers or financial support. I will never forget going to this city to pray one morning and while on the way in the car, I cried out with many tears, "Lord, I am all alone. You must give someone to stand with me." He said to me, "Until you can stand alone with Me, I cannot add anyone to you." Immediately my heart cried out by the help of the Holy Spirit, "Lord Jesus, You are more than enough for me." He then said, "This battle is not yours but Mine." All I could do from that moment was praise Him for the privilege of serving Him and seeing Him work mightily. We must all see afresh each day the sufficiency of His grace enabling us to break through every barrier to speak His Word and do His works.

While Paul endured life-threatening, painful opposition against himself, seeking to make him feel inferior as a mere man, he was not moved by these things because inwardly he was assured by the Life-giving Spirit of Jesus Christ that his ability to preach the Gospel was not from himself. Paul reveals how powerful the all-sufficient grace of Jesus is by how in his weaknesses and trials he was enabled with the strength of the Lord Jesus to do His work. Confronted by a power struggle from those who came representing their own strength, he declared, "They say they are servants of Christ? I know I must sound like a madman to even talk like this, but I have served Him far more! I have worked harder, been put in prison more often, been whipped times without number, and faced death again and again. Five different times the Jewish leaders gave me thirty-nine lashes. Three times I was beaten with rods. Once I was stoned. Three times I was shipwrecked. Once I spent a whole night and a day adrift at sea. I have travelled on many long journeys. I have faced danger from rivers and from robbers. I have faced danger from my own people, the Jews, as well as from the Gentiles. I have faced danger in the cities, in the deserts, and on the seas. And I have faced danger from men who claim to be believers but are not. I have worked hard and long, enduring many sleepless nights. I have been hungry and thirsty and have often gone without food. I have shivered in the cold, without enough clothing to keep me warm. Then, besides all this, I have the daily burden of my concern for all the churches. Who is weak without my feeling that weakness? Who is led astray, made to stumble and fall and have his faith hurt, and I am not on fire [with sorrow or indignation]? If I must boast, I would rather boast about the things that show how weak I am. God, the Father of our Lord Jesus, who is worthy of eternal praise, knows I am not lying, when I tell you that Jesus said to me, My grace (My favour and loving-kindness and mercy) is enough for you [sufficient against any danger and enables you to bear the trouble manfully]; for My strength and power are made perfect (fulfilled and completed) and show themselves most effective in [your] weakness" (2 Corinthians 11:23-31 NLT, 12:9 AMPC).

What am I saying to you? Jesus would have you in such a place of His grace, like the Apostle Paul, that your life on earth would seem meaningless unless it is spent in the joy of doing the work assigned you, the work of telling others the Good News, and doing that only by the grace, strength and ability He supplies. Jesus said, "all of us must quickly carry out the tasks assigned us by the One who sent Me, for there is little time left before the night falls and all work comes to an end" (John 9:4-5 TLB).

I find living in His grace most wonderful. It has helped me to get through every valley and to surmount every mountain. Kathryn Kuhlman, a woman of God through whom Jesus was able to demonstrate His Life, His love and power to heal, once said, "I walked a mile with pleasure and it chattered all the way but left me none the wiser for all it had to say, but then I walked with sorrow and what I learned that day when sorrow walked with me." I remember in 1998, I was weeping before the Lord for many hours because of an intense pain in my soul. Jesus said to me, "If you love Me, keep doing what I have told you, for so you will be filled with My joy. Yes, your joy will overflow!" (John 15:11). As I arose from my knees to get on with the work He has given me, His joy filled my soul and made me whole. Nothing can compare with His joy - the joy of the Lord is my strength!

Follow My Example

I pray that you can see what Paul means when He says that men must consider us Apostles, as servants of Christ and stewards of the mysteries of God (1 Corinthians 4:1). An essential requirement of stewards is that they are found faithful - that they do what their Master tells them to do. Paul says, "What about me? Have I been a good servant? Well, I don't worry over what you think about this or what anyone else thinks. I don't even trust my own opinion on this point. My conscience is clear, but even that isn't final proof. It is the Lord Himself who must examine me and decide. So be careful not to jump to conclusions before the Lord returns as to whether someone is a good servant or not. When the Lord comes, He will turn on the Light so that everyone can see exactly what each one of us is really like, deep down in our hearts. Then everyone will know why we have been doing the Lord's work. At that time God will give to each one whatever praise is coming to him" (1 Corinthians 4:3-5 TLB).

Paul shows that as Christ's Apostles we may never forget that we are examples so that others can learn through us the meaning of the saying, "Follow only what is written in the Scriptures". Paul says this to warn against us becoming more proud of one person than another and entertaining the kind of thinking that exalts self above another. My father, Johan Maasbach, once said to me while I was still young, "Robert, don't forget to humble yourself for it is within every man's heart to exalt self." I can see that one way to daily humble myself is to sweetly serve at home and those who are around me. I also pray daily for the humble meek heart of Jesus to be formed in me by His Spirit and for Jesus to hide me from the praise of men - that men's praise does not touch me - while at the same time showing kindness in appreciation when someone expresses their thanks. Paul completely negates the way of thinking of exalting self over another when he says, "What do you have that was not given to you? And if it was given to you, why do you brag as if you did not receive it as a gift? You think you already have everything you need. You think you are rich. You think you have become kings without us. I wish you really were kings so we could be kings together with you. But it seems to me that God has put us Apostles in the last place, like those sentenced to die. We are like a show for the whole world to see - angels and people. We are fools for Christ's sake, but you are very wise in Christ. We are weak, but you are strong. You receive honour, but we are shamed. Even to this very hour we do not have enough to eat or drink or to wear. We are often beaten, and we have no homes in which to live. We work hard with our own hands for our food. When people curse us, we bless them. When they hurt us, we put up with it. When they tell evil lies about us, we speak nice words about them. Even today, we are treated as though we were the rubbish of the world - the filth of the earth. I am not trying to make you feel ashamed when I say these things. I am writing this to give you a warning as my own dear children. For though you may have ten thousand teachers in Christ, you do not have many fathers. Through the Good News I became your father in Christ Jesus, so I beg you, please follow my example. That is why I am sending to you Timothy, my son in the Lord. I love Timothy, and he is faithful. He will help you remember my way of Life in Christ Jesus, just as I teach it in all the churches everywhere" (1 Corinthians 4:7-17 NCV).

"I have no one like Timothy [no one of so kindred a spirit] who will be so genuinely interested in your welfare and devoted to your interests. For the others all seek [to advance] their own interests, not those of Jesus Christ (the Messiah). But Timothy's tested worth you know, how as a son with his father he has toiled with me zealously in [serving and helping to advance] the Good News (of the Gospel)" (Philippians 2:20-22 AMPC).

All Christ's Apostles are servants of Christ and entrusted by Him with the mysteries of God. In the above scriptures Paul shows, in the way he lives as a representative of Jesus, how important it is not to go beyond what is written but to always be an example in all we go through in this life. As a great Apostle of Christ, Smith Wigglesworth used to say, "Don't waste a great trail for this is your robing time, it is you coming into your inheritance." In other words, this is a perfect opportunity for everyone to see Jesus in you. Be assured that the self-sacrificial, loving, humble heart of Jesus that you see He formed in Paul and Timothy by His Spirit, He gives to live in you as well; for the servant heart of Jesus is what lies at the root of what makes anyone His Apostle.

The Mysteries of God

What did Paul mean by "the mysteries of God"? In Jesus, God unveils His plan for men, which means Jesus embodies His plan. In Jesus, Who is our Life, God unveils all He has prepared for us. Christ is the mystery that Christ's Apostles are given to make known, for in Jesus all the treasures of divine wisdom (comprehensive insight into the ways and purposes of God) and all the riches of spiritual knowledge and enlightenment are stored up and lie hidden (Colossians 2:3 AMPC). With the help of the Holy Spirit, Paul magnificently explains this in his Divinely inspired writings, thereby showing that grace has been given to Christ's Apostles to make known the mystery - the secret plan of God's will - and that this is something God planned from the beginning, according to His good pleasure which He purposed in Himself.

Now this is God's plan, that in the dispensation of the fullness of the times He might gather together in One all things in Christ, both which are in heaven and which are on earth - in Him (Ephesians 1:9-10). In other words, from the beginning God has chosen us all to be His own, united with Him in Jesus. No more barriers, no more separation between heaven and earth. We are all made One with the Father through the Son! Let this thought flood your heart: you are predestined to enjoy the inheritance that is incorruptible and undefiled and does not fade away, reserved in heaven for you in Jesus. The inheritance is the Eternal Life of Sonship you see in Jesus - a Life that proceeds from the Father, a Life of perfect righteousness, peace and joy.

I pray that your heart is filled to overflowing with the Holy Spirit, so that you can see the future you are called to in Jesus. That you can see that He is your ever-living hope, living in your heart by His Spirit, giving you the blessed assurance of faith that for the glory of His accomplished work, He will bring you safely to the Father and present you before Him holy, acceptable and well pleasing in His sight - so that through all eternity the Father may point to you to show who He is in His goodness and mercy in all He has done for you in Jesus.

It is because of this glorious, eternal, ever-living hope we have in Jesus that Christ's Apostles know that the Christian Life we live on earth in these dying bodies is but a foretaste, a down-payment of the Life Jesus has with the Father, and that when we see Him, in the twinkling of an eye we will be changed and made perfect in His likeness. At that moment He will transform our lowly body that it may be conformed to His glorious body, according to the working of His power by which He is able even to subdue and conform all things to Himself. And He Who has prepared us for this is God, Who also has given us the Spirit as a guarantee or down-payment of this new Life (1 Corinthians 15:52; Philippians 3:21; 2 Corinthians 5:5).

I find this all so wonderful! No wonder Christ's Apostles could speak of nothing but the riches of glory we have in

Jesus! Just think for a moment how great the power of His Life-giving Spirit is, that though we are dead in sin, we are made alive with Him. Even though we still live in these dying bodies, Jesus has made us partakers of His Divine nature, by which we escape and live free from the corruption that is in this world through lust. Jesus has saved us by giving us a new birth through His indwelling Life. And He is saving us continuously by the washing of regeneration and by the renewing work of the Holy Spirit, Whom He pours out on us abundantly so that as He lives, we may live also in this world. And He will save us when we see Him, when through the brightness of His glory He conforms our lowly body to be like His glorious body so that forever we are made perfect in His likeness (Titus 3:4-7; John 14:19; Romans 8:23; 1 John 4:17; 3:2). This just makes me want to shout, "Glory! Glory! Glory to God in the highest! Peace on earth and goodwill toward all men! For to you this day is born in the city of David a Saviour Christ Jesus, the Lord!" (Luke 2:14,11).

Selah.
Take a moment and worshipfully meditate on this and the Holy Spirit will refresh you in your union with the Father and the Son, who is Jesus Christ our Lord.

Chapter 18

BUILDING ON
THE RIGHT FOUNDATION

Paul was always compelled by the Spirit of Christ in Him to contend for the defence and confirmation of the Gospel. In one of his most pressing letters he uncharacteristically starts within the first few verses by saying, "I marvel that you are turning away so soon from Him who called you in the grace of Christ, to a different Gospel, which is not another; but there are some who trouble you and want to pervert the Gospel of Christ. But even if we, or an angel from heaven, preach any other Gospel to you than what we have preached to you, let him be accursed. As we have said before, so now I say again, if anyone preaches any other Gospel to you than what you have received, let him be accursed. My little children, for whom I labour in birth again until Christ is formed in you, I would like to be present with you now and to change my tone; for I have doubts about you" (Galatians 1:6-9, 4:19-20).

Paul continues in the same passion of Christ when interceding in one of his other letters saying, "Oh, that you would bear with me in a little folly - and indeed you do bear with me. For I am jealous for you with godly jealousy. For I have betrothed you to one husband, that I may present you as a chaste virgin to Christ. But I fear, lest somehow, as the serpent deceived Eve by his craftiness, so your minds may be corrupted from the simplicity that is in Christ. For if he who comes preaches another Jesus whom we have not preached, or if you receive a different spirit which you have not received, or a different Gospel which you have not accepted - you may well put up with it!" (2 Corinthians 11:1-4).

I pray you can see the weight of responsibility that all Christ's Apostles bear, each in their own day, to declare the Gospel in the demonstration of the Spirit's power so that the faith of the Church rests not on the wisdom of man, lest the cross of Christ should be made of no effect. Considering all this, it is for the spiritual growth of the Church that Paul says, "I determined not to know anything among you except Jesus Christ, and Him crucified, for the kingdom of God is not in word but in power." In other words, the Church is spiritually alive and thereby able to know, perceive and recognise God in and among themselves and be continually conformed to Christ's image, because of the Spirit and power Jesus supplies through His atoning death and resurrection Life at the Father's right hand. Now when I say "Spirit and power" I am thinking of the precious blood of Jesus that is so powerful that it breaks through every barrier that separates men from God. Don't forget that once we were spiritually dead, separated from God, lost and without hope. We were the same as all other people, suffering under the control of the evil influence of satan, because like them we followed the inclination of our sinful nature and therefore by nature were under God's wrath. But God, who is rich in mercy, so that He might satisfy the great love with which He loves us, has drawn us to Himself. He has delivered us out of the control and the dominion of darkness and transferred us into the kingdom of the Son of His love, in Whom we now have redemption the forgiveness of sins.

I therefore plead with you to think how great the power of the blood of Jesus is - as by His Eternal Spirit, His own pre-existent divine personality, He offered Himself an unblemished sacrifice to purchase us for God. And because of His perfect sacrifice, His blood gives Jesus the right to justify us freely by giving and maintaining His Life in us. This is the amazing grace we have the privilege to make known through the Gospel. Just think about this, that because of the blood of Jesus, the Holy Spirit is now continuously at work in us, cleansing our hearts from consciousness of sin and enabling and empowering us to know, perceive and recognise inwardly the only true living God, our heavenly Father, so that we may worship Him in truth as our spirit is made alive with Jesus.

What I want you to see, is that through our union with Jesus He not only strips from every side of us the sins that envelop us and takes them away, but also, through the knowledge of Himself which He possesses, imparts, and maintains in us by His Spirit, He transforms our inclination, changing our motivation to be dead indeed to sin - to inwardly shun sin - and instead be alive to God with an inward desire to please Him. The Holy Spirit wants you to see within yourself that because of everything Jesus has accomplished through the one sacrifice of Himself, a sacrifice that never needs to be repeated, He has forever completely cleansed, made righteous and perfected you who are now consecrated, dedicated, separated, and made holy in Him.

Because this is all so glorious and takes time for your faith to grasp, it bears repeating again and again. This one sacrifice of Himself is so perfect and powerful that it avails and prevails for all time, because after Jesus established the cleansing of our sins in His own blood, fully cleared our record, liberated us from every curse and carried away our weaknesses, our infirmities; when He in Himself bore away our diseases; He, according to the Spirit of holiness, was openly designated the Son of God in power - in a striking, triumphant and miraculous manner - by His resurrection from the dead and ascension to the Father's right hand, where He sat down at His Majesty on High, waiting until

His enemies are made a stool beneath His feet. God, having highly exalted Jesus, has given Him the name which is above every name, that at the name of Jesus every knee should bow, of those in heaven, and of those on earth, and of those under the earth, and that every tongue should confess that Jesus Christ is Lord, to the glory of God the Father (Hebrews 10:11-14; Matthew 8:16-17; Romans 1:4; Psalm 110:1; Philippians 2:9-11).

There is therefore now salvation, righteousness, sanctification, redemption, healing, the baptism in the Holy Spirit and fire - yes, every good and perfect gift from the Father above in no other name but the name of Jesus.

Through Christ Alone

Can you now see why through the covenant in the blood of Jesus, the Gospel which Christ's Apostles preach is the power of God unto salvation? And why the Gospel gives such unshakable certainty and blessed assurance? The new covenant in the blood of Jesus is so powerful, active, and alive that we now live free from the law of sin and death, free from every curse because we are cleansed, renewed, and made alive inwardly, daily to live as He lives.

I know that I keep repeating how powerful this covenant is, but then again, can we ever say enough of such riches and glory? Just think about this, we are now no longer those who by nature deserve God's wrath, and we no longer suffer His judgment by being spiritually dead and separated from Him; but having been made alive with Jesus, who faithfully fulfils God's will by exerting the power of His Resurrection Life over and in us, we are now justified freely by God's grace, so we are no longer under any kind of curse but are blessed with every blessing. Oh, how the Holy Spirit yearns within you to believe the Truth - Jesus has set you free, you are no longer under condemnation, but you are reconciled, made accepted and well-pleasing to the Father, in the beloved - in Jesus.

We therefore no longer live in fear of the Day of Judgment, as it has been appointed to all men to die once and then face the judgment, but we know Jesus was offered once to bear the sins of many. He who pours His love into our hearts by His Spirit afresh each day has set us free from fear so that now we are no longer afraid of what will happen when we appear before God, for we have His Spirit in us crying, "Abba Father!". Therefore with inexpressible joy and full of glory, we eagerly await the coming of Jesus, who will appear a second time, not to deal with our sins, but to complete and bring to fullness our salvation as He presents us to the Father, perfect in Himself - all to the glory of His accomplished work as our Lord and Saviour (Hebrews 9:27-28).

I pray as you read this that the Holy Spirit shows you why Christ's Apostles contend for the Gospel as the only means of salvation and reconciliation for all men, and why Paul so gloriously says, "Jesus is our Life. I have been crucified with Christ; it is no longer I who live, but Christ lives in me; and the Life which I now live in the flesh I live by faith in the Son of God, who loved me and gave Himself for me" (Ephesians 2:1-10; Romans 8:2; Colossians 3:4; Galatians 2:20).

Only by the Blood of Jesus

While writing all this it is hard not to overemphasise the importance for Christ's Apostles to demonstrate through the Gospel that we who are alive with Christ's Life in us have been baptised into His death. This means that the power by which Jesus laid down His Life is now in us enabling us to lay aside the old cursed nature of sin. Sin is therefore no longer our master because Jesus has set us free. His sinless Life in us is our freedom!

I love the way the Holy Spirit speaks through Isaiah when he says, "Lord, You will ordain peace (God's favour and blessings, both temporal and spiritual) for us, for You have also wrought in us and for us all our works. O Lord, our God, other masters besides You have ruled over us, but we will acknowledge and mention Your name only. They [the former tyrant masters] are dead. They shall not live and reappear; they are powerless ghosts, they shall not rise and come back. Therefore, You have visited and made an end of them and caused every memory of them [every trace of their supremacy] to perish" (Isaiah 26:12-14 AMPC).

Oh, what a glorious Gospel to know that Jesus Christ has destroyed sin's power from being able to reign in or over us ever again. His Life now reigns in us, empowering us to put on, to be clothed, to embody His Holy, sinless heavenly Life. Paul says, "This I say, therefore, and testify in the Lord, that you should no longer walk as the rest of the Gentiles walk, in the futility of their mind, having their understanding darkened, being alienated from the Life of God, because of the ignorance that is in them, because of the blindness of their heart; who, being past feeling, have given themselves over to lewdness, to work all uncleanness with greediness. But you have not so learned Christ, if indeed you have heard Him and have been taught by Him, as the Truth is in Jesus: that you put off, concerning your former conduct, the old man which grows corrupt according to the deceitful lusts, and be renewed in the spirit of your mind, and that you put on the new man which was created according to God, in true righteousness and holiness" (Ephesians 4:17-24).

I pray that you will daily, "Clothe yourselves with the new [spiritual self], which is [ever in the process of being] renewed and remoulded into [fuller and more perfect knowledge upon] knowledge after the image (the likeness) of Him Who created it" (Colossians 3:10 AMPC).

Can you see that all Christ's Apostles are ministers of the new covenant? They have a new spiritual mindset for they minister in a new creation anointing - the power of the age to come. This means that through the Spirit of Life in Christ they empower and enable those to whom they minister to live as He lives; whereby they make known the grace of God in all we are freely given in Jesus. The new covenant has made it possible for God's Word, the ever-living Seed, to live and be ever active in our hearts and minds. The Word alive in us cuts all the way through to where our soul and spirit meet, to where joints and marrow come together, to judge the desires, thoughts, and intent of our heart so that nothing is hidden from the Father - so that we live in the Light of His presence here on earth. And with God's Word alive and active in us, we want what He wants and we know what He wants.

New Heart and a New Mind

Writing this, the fountain of Christ's Life springs up in me with His joy. Just think about this: with this new spiritually alive heart and mind, we love being well-pleasing to the Father; we love being led by His Spirit; we love doing His perfect will as we learn from Jesus to love His righteousness and shun - from within by His Spirit - all wickedness, lawlessness, immorality, greed and evil. We have the spiritual mindset where we know no other spirit but His Spirit and know no other image but His Image. We are One with Him; we are in Him and He is in us (Ezekiel 36:26-27; Romans 8:14; Isaiah 59:21 TLB; Hebrews 1:9).

Through the Gospel, Paul shows that we have become gifts to God that He delights in, and that as part of His sovereign plan we have been chosen from the beginning to be His in Jesus, together with all the saints in glory. This is why Paul says, "I have never stopped thanking God for you. I pray for you constantly, asking God, the glorious Father of our Lord Jesus Christ, to give you wisdom to see clearly and really understand who Jesus Christ is and all that He has done for you. I pray that your hearts are flooded with Light so that you can see something of the future He has called you to share. I want you to realise that God has been made rich because we who are Christ's have been given to Him!"

Paul continues, "I pray that you will begin to understand how incredibly great His power is to help those who believe in Him. It is that same mighty power that raised Christ from the dead and seated Him in the place of honour at God's right hand in heaven, far above any other king or ruler or dictator or leader. Yes, His honour is far more glorious than that of anyone else either in this world or in the world to come. And God has put all things under His feet and made Him the supreme Head of the Church - which is His body, filled with Himself, the Author and Giver of everything everywhere" (Ephesians 1:16-23 TLB).

A Wise Master-builder

In all you have read so far, you can see how important it is for Christ's Apostles to equip the saints. By the grace of God, Paul was a wise master-builder, enabled by Him to lay the foundation of His Church. He says to all those labouring in the ministry of Christ to take heed how they build on this foundation, for he says there is no other foundation anyone can lay than that which is laid, which is Christ Jesus (1 Corinthians 3:10-11).

I pray that you take some time to study and meditate on the next scripture, in which Paul shows Jesus' intention for all those whom He has given to be His Apostles, Prophets, Evangelists, Pastors and Teachers. Jesus has given a clear mandate for the work of the ministry and grace according to the measure of His gift - "for the perfecting and the full equipping of the saints (His consecrated people), [that they should do] the work of ministering toward building up Christ's body (the church), [that it might develop] until we all attain oneness in the faith and in the comprehension of the [full and accurate] knowledge of the Son of God, that [we might arrive] at really mature manhood (the completeness of personality which is nothing less than the standard height of Christ's own perfection), the measure of the stature of the fullness of the Christ and the completeness found in Him. So then, we may no longer be children, tossed [like ships] to-and-fro between chance gusts of teaching and wavering with every changing wind of doctrine, [the prey of] the cunning and cleverness of unscrupulous men, [gamblers engaged] in every shifting form of trickery in inventing errors to mislead. Rather, let our lives lovingly express truth [in all things, speaking truly, dealing truly, living truly]. Enfolded in love, let us grow up in every way and in all things into Him Who is the Head, [even] Christ (the Messiah, the Anointed One). For because of Him the whole body (the Church, in all its various parts), closely joined and firmly knit together by the joints and ligaments with which it is supplied, when each part [with power adapted to its need] is working properly [in all its functions], grows to full maturity, building itself up in love" (Ephesians 4:12-16 AMPC).

Paul never wondered what God called him to in the work of the ministry. He knew from the beginning to the end that God - the Father who is faithful - had called him into fellowship with His Son Jesus Christ (1 Corinthians 1:9). And because he lived in fellowship with Jesus, Paul was never caught up with the latest fashion in teaching. Jesus enabled him to fight a good, worthy, honourable, and noble fight by helping him to stay the course; to keep the faith of the Son of God who loved him and helped him finish the race. At the end of his life on earth Paul said, "You know, from the first day that I came, in what manner I always lived among you, serving the Lord Jesus with all humility, with many tears and trials which happened to me; how I kept back nothing that was helpful, I never shrank from telling you the truth, either publicly or in your homes. I have had one message for Jews and Gentiles alike - the necessity of turning from sin to God through faith in our Lord Jesus Christ" (Acts 20:18-21 TLB).

Paul understood what awaits the soul of everyone who believes in Jesus; he knew the crown of righteousness which the Lord Jesus, the righteous Judge, will give on that Day. He said, "And not to me only, but also to all who have loved His appearing" (2 Timothy 4:8). Paul knew his labour in the Gospel had a rich reward for he says, "What is our hope, or joy, or crown of rejoicing? Is it not even you in the presence of our Lord Jesus Christ at His coming? For you are our glory and joy". "When He comes to be glorified in His saints [on that day He will be made more glorious in His consecrated people], and [He will] be marvelled at and admired [in His glory reflected] in all who have believed [who have adhered to, trusted in, and relied on Him], because our witnessing among you was confidently accepted and believed [and confirmed in your lives]" (1 Thessalonians 2:19; 2 Thessalonians 1:10 AMPC).

Compelled by Christ's Love

The secret for Christ's Apostles to rightly divide the Word of Truth is to live in fellowship with Jesus. Only Jesus can hold you on course and enable you not to become entangled with some wind of doctrine, or some power struggle from those who are not Apostles, who are not sent by Jesus, who do not represent Him but seek only their own honour by advancing their own interests and not those of Jesus Christ our Lord.

Paul said, "Brethren, join in following my example, and note those who so walk, as you have us for a pattern. For many walk, of whom I have told you often, and now tell you even weeping, that they are the enemies of the cross of Christ: whose end is destruction, whose god is their belly, and whose glory is in their shame - who set their mind on earthly things" (Philippians 3:17-19).

"We speak as messengers from God, trusted by Him to tell the truth; we change His message not one bit to suit the taste of those who hear it; for we serve God alone, who examines our hearts' deepest thoughts. Never once did we try to win you with flattery, as you very well know, and God knows we were not just pretending to be your friends so that you would give us money!" (1 Thessalonians 2:4-5 TLB).

"We have renounced disgraceful ways (secret thoughts, feelings, desires and underhandedness, the methods and arts that men hide through shame); we refuse to deal craftily (to practice trickery and cunning) or to adulterate or handle dishonestly the Word of God, but we state the truth openly (clearly and candidly). And so, we commend ourselves in the sight and presence of God to every man's conscience" (2 Corinthians 4:2 AMPC).

"As for praise, we have never asked for it from you or anyone else, although as Apostles of Christ we certainly had a right to some honour from you. But we were as gentle among you as a mother feeding and caring for her own children. We loved you dearly - so dearly that we gave you not only God's message, but our own lives too" (1 Thessalonians 2:6-8 TLB).

Can you see how the love of Jesus controls and compels His Apostles? Paul says, "God is my witness how greatly I long for you all with the affection of Jesus Christ" (Philippians 1:8). In other words he says, "I tell the truth when I say that my deep feeling of love for you comes straight from the heart of Jesus Himself" (Philippians 1:8 TEV). Christ's Apostles are true Apostles because Christ's immeasurable love yearns within them to represent and present Him. Thus, Paul says, "Whatever we do, it is certainly not for our own profit but because Christ's love controls and compels us now. Since we believe that Christ died for all of us, we should also believe that we have died to the old life we used to live. He died for all so that all who live - having received Eternal Life from Him - might live no longer for themselves, to please themselves, but to spend their lives pleasing Christ who died and rose again for them" (2 Corinthians 5:13-15 TLB).

The Fellowship of His Suffering

The Life of Christ's Apostles stands in reference to the accomplished work of Jesus on the cross. For me this is the sweetest grace of all the graces we have in Jesus - that we are given to unveil, to embody, to set forth and clearly portray Him crucified (Galatians 3:1). I share this not to make a doctrinal point but to enlighten your heart and mind to see how Jesus grants you to share in the fellowship of His sufferings, and thereby He enables you to lay down your life to sweetly and patiently serve others, to bear their burdens, weaknesses, and failures, and so fulfil the law of Christ, which means you love them with His love (Philippians 3:10; Galatians 6:1-2; John 15:9-13).

The grace we are given to represent Jesus is immeasurably glorious because we are given to embody His Eternal Spirit, His own pre-existent divine personality, by which He offered himself as an unblemished sacrifice to show His love for the Father and to demonstrate the Father's love for us, while we were yet sinners. May the blood He shed, and nothing less, be our consecration, dedication, and separation, so that we may clearly portray Jesus crucified for our sins and raised for our justification, so that through the Light of His Life in us - the Gospel - we may share in His joy and open people's eyes and turn them from darkness to Light and from the power of satan to God, so that they may receive forgiveness of sins and an inheritance among all the saints in glory, through faith in Jesus.

Selah.
Take a moment and worshipfully meditate on this and the Holy Spirit will refresh you in your union with the Father and the Son, who is Jesus Christ our Lord.

Chapter 19

WE DO NOT GET DISCOURAGED

A young Apostle called David Brainerd, who was sent by Jesus to evangelise the American Indians in the 1800s, gave his life to reach them as he passed away before he was thirty years old. David once said something that has made a deep impression on me. He said, "I have nothing to do with earth but to labour in it for God."

The Apostle Paul, like David Brainerd, had this same mind of Christ for he was assured through the bountiful supply of the Spirit of Jesus Christ that his labour would prevail toward the saving work of the Gospel. Paul says, "According to my earnest expectation and hope that in nothing I shall be ashamed, but with all boldness, as always, so now also Christ will be magnified in my body, whether by life or by death. For to me, to live is Christ, and to die is gain. But if I live on in the flesh, this will mean fruit from my labour; yet what I shall choose I cannot tell. For I am hard-pressed between the two, having a desire to depart and be with Christ, which is far better. Nevertheless, to remain in the flesh is more needful for you. And being confident of this, I know that I shall remain and continue with you all for your progress and joy of faith" (Philippians 1:20-25).

David Brainerd, like all Christ's Apostles, was a man of serious prayer. For him, prayer was the mainstream of his Life in the Spirit and his labour in the Gospel. David prayed day and night, crying, "Oh Lord, how I long for more self-mortification, self-denial and humility."

Jesus said, "Learn of Me, for I am gentle (meek) and humble (lowly) in heart, and you will find rest (relief and ease and refreshment and recreation and blessed quiet) for your souls" (Matthew 11:29 AMPC). Jesus will have you in such a place of His grace, where His meek and humble heart is in you to give you continual access to His rich resources, so that you will come short in no gift or ability to do His perfect will, living in His refreshing rest, while you minister in the Gospel.

David Brainerd understood this. He knew that with a pagan and unskilled interpreter by his side, not to mention his own many painful ailments, he could do nothing. He knew that Christ's Life-giving Spirit had to be revealed in him to convince these savage Indians of the truth of the Gospel, or his mission would be in vain. He knew he could not persuade them with human wisdom but only by a demonstration of the love and power of Jesus Christ.

Paul said that to this end all Christ's Apostles labour, "striving according to His working which works in them mightily, warning every man and teaching every man in all wisdom, that they may present every man (to the Father) perfect in Christ Jesus" (Colossians 1:28-29).

Overcoming Discouragement

My prayer is that, like David Brainerd, you will long for more self-mortification, self-denial and humility through your union with Jesus, so that His meek and humble heart will be formed in you by His Spirit; so that it is no longer self that lives but Christ in you. This is very important because in your natural nature you are vulnerable to discouragement, which if this is not overcome by the power of Christ's Life-giving Spirit in you, can distort or veil the Gospel from those whom satan has blinded. Veiled means that they cannot see in you what you are talking about.

The kind of discouragement I am talking about is the gravity of the sin nature that seeks to pull you down and makes you feel separated from God, without hope, harassed by satan with such feelings of despair and powerlessness as if you are still lost, spiritually blind and dead. But we can overcome this because we know the truth that the Father has delivered us from such feelings of discouragement for He has drawn us to Himself out of the control and the dominion of darkness and has transferred us into the kingdom of the Son of His love (Colossians 1:12-13 AMPC).

Therefore like David Brainerd - who through his daily prayer life let his roots grow deep into Christ Himself, daily drawing his nourishment for Life and Godliness from his union with Him - so all Christ's Apostles must know that their ministry is the Life-giving Spirit of Jesus Christ with Whom we are made alive, and by Whom we are qualified and made fit to share the portion which is the inheritance of the saints, God's holy people in the Light. Paul by the Holy Spirit unveils what we have freely received in Jesus. And this is so wonderful and such a miracle of God's grace that it is impossible for Christ's Apostles not to make this known in all its riches of glory and power.

Just think about it, Paul who called himself the chief of sinners and was so painfully bound by sin under the power of the law, he out of all people says, "Where the Spirit of the Lord is, there is liberty." Or, as Jesus would say, "Whom the Son sets free is free indeed" - free from sin. (John 8:36).

Paul shows that Christ's Apostles are given the ministry to set men free from the law of sin and death through the law of Life in Christ, and to demonstrate what this freedom looks like. Paul shows that the Spirit of the Lord Jesus in you is like a mirror that reflects His glory as seen in the Word of God, and that by His Spirit in you, you are constantly being transfigured into His image in ever-increasing splendour and degree of His glory (2 Corinthians 3:17-18; Colossians 3:10 AMPC). This is then also why the Apostle Paul says, "Since we hold and engage in this ministry of the Spirit by the mercy of God [granting us favour, benefits, opportunities, and especially salvation], we do not get discouraged (spiritless and despondent with fear) or become faint with weariness and exhaustion" (2 Corinthians 4:1-2 AMPC).

My Peace I give to you

I pray that you can see now that the Father has made you one with Jesus; that you are being renewed with His Life-giving Spirit in the inward man daily, and thereby empowered not to give way to that downward pull of the sin nature and those demonic feelings of anxiety, despair and discouragement. The Holy Spirit will continually remind you that because Christ's Life-giving Spirit is in you, satan has nothing in you, nothing in common with you. There is nothing in you that belongs to him - satan has no power over you, for sin is no longer your master! Christ's righteousness now reigns in you by His Spirit. This means that Jesus is upholding you with His own righteousness, the righteousness He enjoys in the presence of the Father, and He will not in any way fail you nor give you up nor leave you without support.

Jesus says, "[I will] not, [I will] not, [I will] not in any degree leave you helpless nor forsake, nor let [you] down, (relax My hold on you)! [Assuredly not!]" So you can take comfort and be very encouraged and confidently and boldly say, "The Lord is my Helper; I will not be seized with alarm. [I will not fear or dread or be terrified.] What can man do to me?" (Hebrews 13:5-6 AMPC; Joshua 1:5; Psalm 27:1, 118:6).

Jesus says, "Peace I leave with you; My [own] peace I now give and bequeath to you. Not as the world gives do I give to you. Do not let your hearts be troubled, neither let them be afraid. [Stop allowing yourselves to be agitated and disturbed; and do not permit yourselves to be fearful and intimidated and cowardly and unsettled.]" You see, through Jesus the peace of God, which surpasses all understanding, is now guarding your hearts and minds (John 14:27 AMPC; Philippians 4:7).

Arise and Shine!

It is very important that you remember where your help comes from! God has said, "Arise! [from the depression and prostration in which circumstances have kept you - rise to a New Life]! Shine (be radiant with the glory of the Lord), for your Light has come, and the glory of the Lord has risen upon you! For behold, darkness shall cover the earth, and dense darkness [all] peoples, but the Lord shall arise upon you [O Jerusalem], and His glory shall be seen on you. And nations shall come to your Light, and kings to the brightness of your rising" (Isaiah 60:1-3 AMPC).

Jesus is the Light of Life Who has come to give the Light of His Life to shine in your heart. As Paul so powerfully says, "God Who said, 'Let Light shine out of darkness', has shone in our hearts so as [to beam forth] the Light for the illumination of the knowledge of the majesty and glory of God [as it is manifest in the Person and is revealed] in the face of Jesus Christ (the Messiah). However, we possess this precious treasure [the divine Light of the Gospel] in [frail, human] vessels of earth, that the grandeur and exceeding greatness of the power may be shown to be from God and not from ourselves. So that we may proclaim the praises of Him who called us out of darkness into His marvellous Light" (2 Corinthians 4:6-7 AMPC; 1 Peter 2:9).

With due respect for the suffering caused by the powers of darkness that engulf so many, I can boldly say - together with all Christ's Apostles - that the Light of Christ's Life has broken the power of darkness. "The Light of Christ's Life shines on in the darkness and the darkness has never overpowered it [put it out, absorbed it or appropriated it, and is unreceptive to it]" (John 1:5 AMPC).

Paul says, "Once you were darkness, but now you are Light in the Lord; walk as children of Light [lead the lives of those native-born to the Light]. For the fruit (the effect, the product) of the Light or the Spirit [consists] in every form of kindly goodness, uprightness of heart, and trueness of Life. And try to learn [in your experience] what is pleasing to the Lord [let your lives be constant proofs of what is most acceptable to Him]. Take no part in and have no fellowship with the fruitless deeds and enterprises of darkness, but instead [let your lives be so in contrast as to] expose and reprove and convict them. For it is a shame even to speak of or mention the things that [such people] practice in secret."

"Therefore, let no foul or polluting language, nor evil word nor unwholesome or worthless talk [ever] come out of your mouth, but only such [speech] as is good and beneficial to the spiritual progress of others, as is fitting to the need and the occasion, that it may be a blessing and give grace (God's favour) to those who hear it. And do not grieve the Holy Spirit of God [do not offend or vex or sadden Him], by Whom you were sealed (marked, branded as God's own, secured) for the day of redemption (of final deliverance through Christ from evil and the consequences of sin). Let all bitterness and indignation and wrath (passion, rage, bad temper) and resentment (anger, animosity) and quarrelling (brawling, clamour, contention) and slander (evil-speaking, abusive or blasphemous language) be banished from you, with all malice (spite, ill will, or baseness of any kind)."

"And become useful and helpful and kind to one another, tender-hearted (compassionate, understanding, loving-hearted), forgiving one another [readily and freely], as God in Christ forgave you" (Ephesians 5:8-12, 4:29-32 AMPC).

Stand Firm in His Might

I hereby remind you to guard against letting satan get a grip on you by twisting your thoughts. Remember that during the last supper, satan had already put the thought of betraying Jesus in the heart of Judas Iscariot (John 13:21, 26-27). And remember that Peter said to Ananias, "Why did you let satan rule your thoughts to lie to the Holy Spirit and to keep for yourself part of the money you received for the land?" (Acts 5:3 NCV). You can see how important it is to stay vigilant by the Spirit of Christ in you so you can stand against the devil's mind-orientated strategies. Give the devil no place, resist him by being steadfast in faith and he will flee from you!

My dear wife Virginia once said to me, "We do spiritual warfare by living holy." I agree completely that as we live one with Jesus in spirit, soul, and body, we have all we need in Him to fend off the evil one, for the Life-giving Spirit of Jesus carefully watches over and protects us. Christ's divine presence within us preserves us against the evil one, and therefore he is not able to lay hold or get a grip on us (1 John 5:18). I pray that in your Apostolic commission you know that the Lord Jesus is faithful and that He will make you strong and guard you from satanic attacks of every kind (2 Thessalonians 3:3 TLB).

King David declares, "Your God has commanded your strength [your might in His service and impenetrable hardness to temptation]; O God, display Your might and strengthen what You have wrought for us!" For in the day when I called, You answered me; and You strengthened me with strength (might and inflexibility to temptation) in my inner self" (Psalm 68:28, 138:3 AMPC).

When Paul encountered satanic opposition and harassment in his Apostolic commission to share the Gospel, he prayed three times asking Jesus to remove this. Jesus gave Paul a most important unveiling response when He said, "My grace (My favour and loving-kindness and mercy) is enough for you [sufficient against any danger and enables you to bear the trouble manfully]; for My strength and power are made perfect (fulfilled and completed) and show themselves most effective in [your] weakness." Therefore, Paul says, "Most gladly I will rather boast in my infirmities, that the power of Christ may rest upon me, (yes, may pitch a tent over me). I take pleasure in infirmities, in reproaches, in needs, in persecutions, in distresses, for Christ's sake. For when I am weak, then I am strong" (2 Corinthians 12:9-10 AMPC).

The reality and power of Christ's Life became the armour in which the Apostle Paul could do his most important work of making known the Gospel in a dark, sighing, dying world filled with multitudes of precious souls who so need Jesus to save them. He shows that to be clothed with Christ provides us with the full armour by which we have all we need to live like Him, share the Gospel and stand firm in an evil day (Ephesians 6:10-18).

Clothed with Jesus

Just as we get dressed each day, so we should put on the Lord Jesus Christ, for He is the armour of Light. Clothed with His Life, our weak human nature is hidden and protected in whatever environment we encounter (Romans 13:12-14). Jesus said, "I counsel you to buy from Me white garments, that you may be clothed, that the shame of your nakedness may not be revealed" (Revelations 3:18). What Jesus is saying is that when we daily invest in Him, feed on Him, draw our nourishment for Life and Godliness from our union with Him, we shall be found in Him, clothed with His Life-giving Spirit, so that our natural human nature is hidden with Him in the bosom, the intimate presence of the Father, so that we are more conscious of Him than ourselves and represent Him in all we are, say and do (Colossians 3:3).

This is a marvellous mystery which we see foreshadowed in Genesis, when Adam and Eve were the first to suffer the pains of sin and feel the awful loneliness of being self-conscious instead of God-conscious, exposed to the environment instead of being Masters over it. God immediately showed the wonder of His redeeming love by clothing Adam and Eve with the skin of an animal whose blood was shed to cover them. This was something that became known as atonement, meaning "to cover, to appease, to redeem - that is, to buy you free from the painful consequences of sin". What God did for Adam and Eve is an example of what He has done for us in Jesus.

While I would love to expound this at length as it is such a large revelation in scripture, I ask you to daily look to Jesus, Who was clothed with and by God in the body He prepared for Him; for in Jesus we see what we are predestined to be, since He is the fullness of the Godhead in a human body.

My heart overflows with the love of Jesus as I write these things, and I therefore pray that you are filled with His love as you consider that you are in Him, made full and having come to fullness of Life [in Christ you too are filled with the Godhead - Father, Son and Holy Spirit - and reach full spiritual stature] (Colossians 2:9-10 AMPC). What you see in Jesus must be in all the Church, as we are His body, the fullness of Him who fills us all with all of Himself (Ephesians 1:23).

An Incarnation not an Imitation

People said of the old praying saints that when they came out of prayer their faces were radiant with Christ's glory. My father, Johan Maasbach, was a great Apostle of the Lord Jesus Christ. In 1951 he wrote a letter to my mother (who at this time of writing is still with us on earth and is one of those glorious saints in whom the Life of Christ is most beautifully embodied) saying; "Christian Life is a Christ Life. It is not an imitation; but an incarnation." I plead with you that while you are still in this temporal body, that you clothe yourself each day with the Lord Jesus, so that the nakedness of your human nature may not be exposed but hidden in Him.

Just as the police, armed forces or medics clothe themselves in their uniforms to represent the authority entrusted to them, so you. As Paul says, "Have clothed yourselves with the new [spiritual self], which is [ever in the process of being] renewed and remoulded into [fuller and more perfect knowledge upon] knowledge after the image (the likeness) of Him Who created it."

I pray the Holy Spirit so unveils this in you that you daily put on the Lord Jesus Christ! And that you "clothe yourselves, as God's own chosen ones (His own picked representatives), [who are] purified and holy and well-beloved [by God Himself, by putting on behaviour marked by] tender-hearted pity and mercy, kind feeling, a lowly opinion of yourselves, gentle ways, [and] patience [which is tireless and long-suffering, and has the power to endure whatever comes, with good temper]. Be gentle and forbearing with one another and, if one has a difference (a grievance or complaint) against another, readily pardoning each other; even as the Lord has [freely] forgiven you, so must you also [forgive]. And above all these [put on] love and enfold yourselves with the bond of perfectness [which binds everything together completely in ideal harmony]. And let the peace (soul harmony which comes) from Christ rule (act as umpire continually) in your hearts [deciding and settling with finality all questions that arise in your minds, in that peaceful state] to which as [members of Christ's] one body you were also called [to live]. And be thankful (appreciative), [giving praise to God always]" (Colossians 3:10, 12-15 AMPC).

Always remember that the Church is the body of Christ. It is the completion of Him Who Himself completes all things everywhere as He fills us all with all of Himself.

Considering all this, I charge you therefore in the Lord Jesus to daily read the Scriptures and listen to them narrated. Submerge yourself in the Word day and night and pray, worship and praise. In other words, live in communion with the Father and the Son, letting the Holy Spirit overflow in you as, with Jesus, you abide in the love of the Father, "so that you may have the power of His Spirit and be strong to apprehend and grasp with all the saints [God's devoted people, the experience of that love] what is the breadth and length and height and depth [of it]; [That you may really come] to know [practically, through experience for yourselves] the love of Christ, which far surpasses mere knowledge [without experience]; that you may be filled [through all your being] unto all the fullness of God [may have the richest measure of the divine Presence, and become a body wholly filled and flooded with God Himself]! Now to Him Who, by (in consequence of) the [action of His] power that is at work within us, is able to [carry out His purpose and] do superabundantly, far over and above all that we [dare] ask or think [infinitely beyond our highest prayers, desires, thoughts, hopes, or dreams] - To God be glory in the church by Christ Jesus throughout all generations forever and ever. Amen (so be it)" (Ephesians 3:18-21 AMPC/NKJ).

Selah.

Take a moment and worshipfully meditate on this and the Holy Spirit will refresh you in your union with the Father and the Son, who is Jesus Christ our Lord.

Chapter 20

RADIANT WITH
THE LIGHT OF HIS LIFE

It is difficult for me to say "in closing" as it is impossible to have covered all the Apostolic fundamentals set before us in the Word of God; and also because I have an earnest desire to share so many more things that are essential for today's Apostles to bear in their God-given ministry. But I know Jesus said that the Holy Spirit will teach you all things, so again I charge you in the Lord Jesus Christ to read His Word and meditate therein day and night. Jesus will never fail to open your understanding by the Holy Spirit to all that is yours in Him.

However, in closing I would like to say a few more things to stir up the pure mind of Christ in you so that you may know the abundant supply of His grace, blessings, favour and gifts. Believe that in the ministry you have received in Jesus, He gives you every gift of the Holy Spirit you need to carry out the work He has entrusted to you. And when I say *every gift,* that is exactly what I mean. Believe that Jesus, by the Holy Spirit, works in you with every gift to do His work so that in all you are, say and do, you represent Him (take some time and meditate on John 1:16 AMPC; 1 Corinthians 1 & 12; Romans 12:6-8).

Paul shows from his own experience how, by the Holy Spirit, Jesus enabled him to do the work He gave him. He says, "I am, by God's grace, a minister of Jesus Christ to you Gentiles, bringing you the Gospel and offering you up as a fragrant sacrifice to God; for you have been made pure and pleasing to Him by the Holy Spirit. I am very grateful for all

Jesus has done through me and would never dare speak of anything except what He has accomplished through me, in word and deed, to make you Gentiles obedient, with mighty signs and wonders, by the power of the Holy Spirit. In this way I have preached the full Gospel of Christ all the way from Jerusalem clear over into Illyricum (Croatia)" (Romans 15:15-19 TLB/NKJV).

Jesus said, "The Comforter (Counsellor, Helper, Intercessor, Advocate, Strengthener, Standby), the Holy Spirit, Whom I will send to you from the Father, [in My place, to represent Me and act on My behalf], the Spirit of Truth Who comes (proceeds) from the Father, He [Himself] will testify regarding Me. He will teach you all things. And He will cause you to recall (will remind you of, bring to your remembrance) everything I have told you. He will honour and glorify Me, because He will take of (receive, draw upon) what is Mine and will reveal (declare, disclose, transmit) it to you."

"Everything that the Father has is Mine. That is what I meant when I said that He [the Holy Spirit] will take the things that are Mine and will reveal (declare, disclose, transmit) it to you" (John 14:26; 15:26; 16:14-15 AMPC).

Believe that in nothing you will fall short of God's glory, but that Jesus will be magnified in your body in both word and deed, with signs and wonders, various miracles and gifts of the Holy Spirit, for there is nothing Jesus has with the Father that He will withhold from you.

Preach the Full Gospel

Just think about how much the Father loves you in all that Jesus did for you while you were yet a sinner, by dying for you. How much more, now that you are His child, will the Father do for you through Christ's Life!

Like a trumpet that gives a clear and undeniable call from the throne of grace - a call that only grows louder and louder to announce the Day of the Lord Jesus' return - so Christ's Apostles go forth throughout the whole earth preaching no other Gospel than that which the Apostle Paul preached when he said, "Now let me remind you of the gospel (the glad tidings of salvation) which I proclaimed to you, which you welcomed and accepted and upon which your faith rests and by which you are saved, if you hold fast and keep firmly what I preached to you, unless you believed at first without effect and all for nothing. For I passed on to you first of all what I also had received, that Christ (the Messiah, the Anointed One) died for our sins in accordance with [what] the Scriptures [foretold], that He was buried, that He arose on the third day as the Scriptures foretold. He was seen by Peter and later by the rest of the Twelve. After that he was seen by more than five hundred Christian brothers at one time, most of whom are still alive, though some have died by now. Then James saw Him, and later all the Apostles. Last of all I saw Him too, long after the others, as though I had been born almost too late for this" (1 Corinthians 15:1-9 AMPC/TLB).

I say all of this to remind you to preach the full Gospel of Christ and not just a part of it. If you preach that Jesus, by offering Himself in His death on the cross, accomplished our freedom from sin and guilt as He fully cleared our record in His own precious blood and after this sat down at the right hand of the divine Majesty on high, but do not also preach in the power of His Life-giving Spirit about the Life He gives so that we may live as He lives in this dying body - the Life that is not our own but a gift of God - then your Gospel will fall short of the fullness of the glory and blessings God gives in Jesus.

Paul makes this unmistakably clear when he says, "If Christ has not been raised, then your faith is useless, and you are still guilty of your sins. In that case, all who have died believing in Christ are lost! And if our hope in Christ is only for this life, we are more to be pitied than anyone in the world" (1 Corinthians 15:17-19 NLT). You see this is the wonder of Christianity - that the Life Jesus now lives, to the glory of God, is what He gives and maintains in us by His Spirit. This Life is a Life of Sonship; it is eternal; it never fades, grows old or dies, for Jesus having been raised from the dead cannot die - death has no dominion over Him. He is the Prince of Life! The Life Jesus gives is a sinless Life for there is no sin in Him. Therefore, you can now live free from sin in Him. The Life He gives is perfectly One with the Father for there is no separation in Jesus from the bright presence of the Father. Jesus is in the Father and the Father is in Him; they are One, and oh what glory, what unsearchable riches, what immeasurable love that we are now united with them in this oneness!

Can you see why His Life in us is the anchor for our soul? It is the blessed assurance and foretaste of glory divine. By the power of His Life in us, God is able to keep us while we are still in our dying body and keep us for the fullness of salvation that will be revealed when we see Jesus and receive a body like His. We believers in Christ, who have the first fruits of the Spirit, groan inwardly as we eagerly await our adoption, the redemption of our bodies, for in hope we were saved (Romans 8:23-24). Jesus will appear a second time for those who eagerly look for His appearing to bring to fullness our salvation in Him (Hebrews 9:28)!

Living as More than Conquerors

When the Church looks to Him only for the things in this life, its faith will be weak. But when like the saints of old, we know we have a better and lasting reward awaiting in His presence, we will not give up our confidence of faith which has a great recompense of reward even in the face of trials, tribulations and death (Hebrews 10:32-39).

Paul, who was no stranger to trials and tribulations, said, "I think you ought to know, dear brothers, about the hard time we went through in Asia. We were really crushed and overwhelmed and feared we would never live through it. We felt we were doomed to die and saw how powerless we were to help ourselves; but that was good, for then we put everything into the hands of God, who alone could save us, for He can even raise the dead. And He did help us, and saved us from a terrible death; yes, and we expect Him to do it again and again" (2 Corinthians 1:8-10 TLB).

Through the Holy Spirit, Paul shows the magnificence of God having predestined us to be conformed to the image of His Son Jesus, so that He might be the firstborn among many brethren. Just think about this, that having been predestined to be conformed to His image, He has now also called us, justified us and given us to share His glory by His Spirit in us.

"What then shall we say to these things? If God is for us, who can be against us? He who did not spare His Own Son, but delivered Him up for us all, how shall He not with Him also freely give us all things? Who dares accuse us whom God has chosen for His own? Will God? No! He is the One who has forgiven us and given us right standing with Himself. Who then will condemn us? Will Christ? No! For He is the One who died for us and came back to Life again for us and is sitting at the place of highest honour next to God, pleading for us there in heaven. Who then can ever keep Christ's love from us? When we have trouble or calamity, when we are hunted down or destroyed, is it because He doesn't love us anymore? And if we are hungry or penniless or in danger or threatened with death, has God deserted us? No, for the Scriptures tell us that for His sake we must be ready to face death at every moment of the day. We are like sheep awaiting slaughter, but despite all this, overwhelming victory is ours, for in all these things we are more than conquerors through Christ who loved us enough to die for us. I am convinced that nothing can ever separate us from His love. Death can't, and life can't. The angels won't, and all the powers of hell itself cannot keep God's love away. Our fears for today, our worries about tomorrow, or where we are - high above in the sky, or in the deepest ocean - nothing will ever be able to separate us from the love of God demonstrated by our Lord Jesus Christ when He died for us on the cross" (Romans 8:31-39 NKJV/TLB).

I pray that right now while you are reading this, the Holy Spirit fills and floods your heart with the love of the Father and Jesus Christ our Lord and Saviour. I pray that you will bless the Lord Jesus at all times, no matter what you are going through - let His praise forever be on your lips (Psalm 34)!

Bringing Light into Darkness

Paul and Silas, despite being beaten, bleeding, and in chains - with their feet fastened in stocks - were praying and singing hymns to God while the other prisoners were listening to them. Suddenly, there was such a violent earthquake that the foundations of the prison were shaken. At once all the prison doors flew open, and everybody's chains came loose. The jailer woke up, and when he saw the prison doors open, he drew his sword and was about to take his own life because he thought the prisoners had escaped. But Paul shouted, "Don't harm yourself! We are all here!" (Acts 16:25-28).

Often the test of faith is not just to sing and praise the Lord when things seem impossible, but to stay when a door opens and you could leave. My father and mother, Johan and Wilhelmina Maasbach, started one of the first churches they planted in a city called Gouda, in Holland - the Netherlands. After some years, when it seemed nothing was happening, my mother asked my father if they should move on, but my father responded by saying that they had only been there for seven years and should give the people a chance to repent and be saved. Because they stayed, they saw the Lord Jesus build one of the largest congregations in that city. This was also the city where I was born in 1960. Often Christ's Apostles are called upon to bring salvation to those who are in the darkest and most hopelessly forsaken places. Paul and Silas stayed in the jail, despite the door being open, and were able to share the love of Jesus with the jailer. They led him and his whole family to salvation and water-baptising them before daybreak. I pray that this same Apostolic grace to stay and share the Gospel is in you too.

Remember Jesus said, "The Spirit of the Lord is on Me, because He has anointed Me to preach the Gospel to the poor. He has sent Me to heal the broken-hearted, to proclaim freedom for the prisoners and recovery of sight for the blind, to release the oppressed, to proclaim the year of the Lord's favour" (Luke 4:18-19 NIV/NKJV).

Paul, living and labouring in the anointing of Jesus, said, "Don't ever forget the wonderful fact that Jesus Christ was a Man, born into King David's family; and that He is God, as shown by the fact that He rose again from the dead. It is because I have preached these great truths that I am in trouble here and have been put in jail like a criminal. But the Word of God is not chained, even though I am. I am more than willing to suffer if that will bring salvation and eternal glory in Christ Jesus to those God has chosen" (2 Timothy 2:8-10 TLB).

The Church that was born in the darkness of this prison, where God commanded the Light of His Life to shine through the Gospel embodied in Paul and Silas, shows you that Jesus is equally available to all who call on His name. Believe that where you are right now, the Light of the Gospel will bring Christ's Life to those with whom you share His love.

Jesus said, "You are the light of the world. Let your light so shine before men, (let them see the Light of My Life in you) so that they may see your good works and glorify your Father in heaven" (Matthew 5:14-16).

Singing a New Song

"Because you have been raised to Life with Christ, set your heart on the things that are in heaven, where Christ sits on His throne at the right side of God. Keep your minds fixed on things there, not on things here on earth. For you have died, and your Life is hidden with Christ in God. Your real Life is Christ and when He appears, then you too will appear with Him and share His glory!" (Colossians 3:1-4 TEV).

Now this is the joy set before us in Jesus, that to the glory of His accomplished work we are co-heirs with Him and share His glory as He presents us to the Father - holy, acceptable and well-pleasing in His sight - and we all stand before the Father in One Spirit singing a new song, the song of the redeemed: "'You are worthy for You were slain, and Your blood has bought people from every nation as gifts for God. And You have gathered them into a kingdom and made them priests of our God; they shall reign upon the earth.' Then I heard the singing of millions of angels surrounding the throne and the Living Beings and the Elders: 'The Lamb is worthy' (loudly they sang it!) – 'The Lamb who was slain. He is worthy to receive the power, and the riches, and the wisdom, and the strength, and the honour, and the glory, and the blessing.' And then I heard everyone in heaven and earth, and from the dead beneath the earth and in the sea, exclaiming, 'The blessing and the honour and the glory and the power belong to the One sitting on the throne, and to the Lamb forever and ever.' And the four Living Beings kept saying, 'Amen!' And the twenty-four Elders fell down and worshiped Him" (Revelation 5:9-14 TLB).

Keeping your Eyes on Jesus

It is not possible without repeating the scriptures to give you all that is set before us in Jesus. John the beloved said, "If it were all written down, the whole world would not have room enough for all the books that would be written" (John 21:25). I pray that He who asked me to write this book will use the few thoughts set before you to help you recognise and know the only true Living God in Jesus Christ His Son.

Remember that long ago God spoke in many, different ways to the fathers through the prophets in visions, dreams, and even face-to-face, telling them little by little about His plans. But in these last days He has spoken to us in the person of His Son Jesus, Whom He appointed Heir and lawful Owner of all things, by and through Whom He created the world, the reaches of space and the ages of time, arranging them in order, sustaining and upholding all things by the Word of His power. Jesus Christ, God's Son, shines out with God's glory and all that He is and does marks Him as God. He is the sole expression of the glory of God, the Light-being, the out-raying or radiance of the divine. He is the perfect imprint and very image of God's nature.

Therefore look to Jesus, the Son of God who is the Son of Man - and not just any man, for He is the promised Seed of the woman, the promised Seed of Abraham and the promised Seed of David. He is the Word who became flesh, human, incarnate and tabernacled (as He fixed His tent of flesh) and lived awhile among us in the body God prepared for Him, and we saw His glory - the glory of the One and only, full of grace and truth, for He came forth from the bosom - the intimate presence of the Father - to make Him known in Himself, so that we may all find and know and see the only true living God in Him. And you now have your Life in Him, who is your Life, who gives and maintains His Life in you by His Spirit.

I therefore pray that the Life-giving Spirit of Jesus Christ is continually unveiled in you - in all you are, say and do - for you are in Him made full, and having come to fullness of Life in Christ, you too are filled with the Godhead - Father, Son and Holy Spirit - and reach full spiritual stature. And that God; Who is the Author and the Giver of peace, Who brought again from among the dead our Lord Jesus, that great Shepherd of the sheep, by the blood that sealed, ratified the everlasting agreement, covenant, testament. Strengthen, complete, perfect and make you what you ought to be and equip you with everything good that you may carry out His will; while He Himself works in you and accomplishes that which is pleasing in His sight, through Jesus Christ - the Messiah; to Whom be the glory forever and ever - to the ages of the ages. Amen - so be it (Hebrews 13:20-21 AMPC).

The grace of the Lord Jesus Christ, and the love of God, and the communion of the Holy Spirit be with you. Amen.

Selah.
Take a moment and worshipfully meditate on this and the Holy Spirit will refresh you in your union with the Father and the Son, who is Jesus Christ our Lord.